MENTOR
COACH
to Peak Professional Performance
LEAD

MENTOR
COACH
to Peak Professional Performance
LEAD

LAURIE K. BAEDKE

ACHE Management Series

Library of Congress Cataloging-in-Publication Data is on file at the Library of Congress, Washington, DC.

ISBN: 978-1-64055-381-1

The paper used in this publication meets the minimum requirements of American National Standard for Information Sciences—Permanence of Paper for Printed Library Materials, ANSI Z39.48-1984. ∞ ™

Manuscript editor: Kevin McLenithan; Cover designer: James Slate; Layout: PerfecType

Found an error or a typo? We want to know! Please e-mail it to hapbooks@ache.org, mentioning the book's title and putting "Book Error" in the subject line.

For photocopying and copyright information, please contact Copyright Clearance Center at www.copyright.com or at (978) 750-8400.

Health Administration Press
A division of the Foundation of the
   American College of Healthcare Executives
300 S. Riverside Plaza, Suite 1900
Chicago, IL 60606-6698
(312) 424-2800

Contents

Detailed Contents

Preface

THIS BOOK IS a much-needed examination of the important leadership practices of mentorship, sponsorship, and coaching. It's widely known that these three endeavors are valuable, but as we traverse our career journeys and life in general, we far too often tend to drift away from them, partake of them too infrequently, or fail to integrate them into our own development or the development of others. You see, mentorship, sponsorship, and coaching are bidirectional. By that, I mean that there is nary a season of our lives, personally or professionally, where we do not need to be well mentored, well sponsored, and well coached. And it is incumbent upon us, as leaders, to turn around and serve as mentors, sponsors, and coaches to those around us.

It is my observation, confirmed by an abundance of research, that the most effective leaders "curate their circle," surrounding themselves with sound counsel. They assemble boards of advisors, which help them in the same vital ways that similar governing bodies do for corporations and institutions, enabling them to better steward themselves in life and in leadership. We are well served by having wise individuals around us who share our journey: offering connection and support, lending expertise from their learned experience, sharing power and influence to help us advance, and courageously and candidly offering feedback from their position of objectivity and concern for our continual improvement. This "kitchen cabinet" both equips and encourages us. At some moments, they deliver doses of tough love, challenging and exhorting us or holding us accountable to the goals and standards we've set. At others, they offer empathy and compassion, coming alongside us in more difficult seasons to carry us when we're weary, believe in us when we're struggling to do so ourselves, or simply dust us off and nudge us back into the arena.

Throughout this book, we'll review the myriad reasons why partaking in mentoring practices is vital to our thriving, both individually and organizationally. Mentorship, sponsorship, and coaching result in enhanced development, advancement, and performance, respectively. The resulting positive and powerful outcomes are integral to our achievement of the leadership impact of which we are capable and are necessary for organizations to rise to the endless challenges and opportunities they encounter.

Mentorship, sponsorship, and coaching also contribute to enhanced well-being; improved diversity, equity, inclusion, and belonging; and bolstered bench strength and succession planning. Well-mentored individuals perform at higher levels. They are more creative, innovative, resilient, adaptable, loyal, and satisfied with their lives and careers. They are better prepared for the next levels of leadership; have stronger networks; and are more likely to mentor, sponsor, and coach others. To me, all that reads like a laundry list of the most desirable attributes for a team member, employee, or boss. Wouldn't you agree?

I felt drawn to write this book because I am the immeasurably grateful beneficiary of so many people who have generously invested in me by developing me through mentorship, advancing me through sponsorship, and honing my capacity to thrive in many facets of my life through coaching. In my career journey, I've had many opportunities, both formally and informally, to serve as a mentor, sponsor, and coach to others, and I have found it to be one of the most meaningful and rewarding parts of the work I've been privileged to do.

I began my career as a leader, then an executive, in a traditional healthcare environment before venturing out to start a management consultancy that helps physicians start and manage private practices. Over the years of my entrepreneurial journey, I began receiving opportunities to teach in academic settings as an adjunct faculty member, established a professional speaking practice, and became certified as a leadership coach. Because of my active engagement as a member of the American College of Healthcare Executives (ACHE) and other professional associations, as a board member for my local ACHE chapter, as a member of national committees, and as a content expert and speaker, I naturally became heavily invested in seeking out ways I could surround myself with people who had the experience and expertise to prepare me for and propel me to the next levels of leadership. As others were pouring into me, I felt led to immediately turn around and share that gift with others. Leadership is relational, not transactional, so it is logical that we would approach the pursuit of our own formation in an interdependent fashion that brings flourishing and excellence to the world.

It is my hope that upon reading these chapters, you'll feel encouraged and better equipped to put mentorship, sponsorship, and coaching to work for your edification and that of others around you.

Go forth in growth, my friends.

Acknowledgments

TO MY HUSBAND, Wes, and our amazing children, Sophia and Quinn: I am better because of your unconditional love, encouragement, and example of humility and courage and discipline. I cherish our circle that reflects Proverbs 27:17, which reads, "As iron sharpens iron, so one person sharpens another."

As a leader, I stand on the shoulders of so many giants who have gone before me, shined a light on my path, and shown by their example a model of leadership that has shaped my own. If I tried to name the mentors, sponsors, and coaches who have contributed to my journey, the list would be pages long, and I would never forgive myself for overlooking a treasured colleague. But I must acknowledge by name the leader whose faith in me opened the door for my first executive role in healthcare administration and whose introduction to this amazing organization, the American College of Healthcare Executives, set me on a career path that has been extraordinarily rewarding and fulfilling: Robert L. Omer, LFACHE. Bob, thank you for your most superb example and all that you taught me.

To my inner circle: you know who you are, and I would not be who I am without your endless encouragement, support, example, and advice. I love you dearly.

And last, to all the mentees, sponsees, and coachees who have trusted me as a voice of support, encouragement, exhortation, advice, and wisdom: I cherish the relationships that we've shared and hope that you'll all continue to pay it forward.

CHAPTER 1

Defining Mentorship, Sponsorship, and Coaching

The smooth path to a fruitful mentor-mentee relationship is paved with formal programming.

"Successful" mentoring relationships are as elusive as the Loch Ness monster, unicorns, or Bigfoot.

One either has the fortune of a good mentoring partner—or one doesn't.

THESE COMMONLY HELD beliefs are just the tip of the iceberg when it comes to lingering misconceptions about mentoring. Other untruths are derived from outdated research rooted in the 1970s and mid-1980s, as analyzed by Monica C. Higgins and Kathy E. Kram in their article "Reconceptualizing Mentoring at Work." As Higgins and Kram note, this research "long espoused the benefits of having a mentoring relationship for an individual's personal and professional development." However, with the passage of time, researchers have gleaned considerably more insight into the dynamics and advantages of both traditional mentoring and alternative mentor relationships, which have increasingly entered the public discourse and have an ever-growing body of literature on the subject.

"The phenomenon of mentoring—that is, the provision of career and psychosocial support—is still of primary interest," Higgins and

Kram point out, "but who provides such support and how such support is provided are now more in question." They highlight increasing variance in "development network diversity": a range of social systems (community, employer, school) from which individuals can draw for their mentoring support. This "added complexity" has mirrored changes in other areas of organizational research. There is increasing pressure to be responsive in the face of competitive conditions, keen stakeholder expectations, and clashing structural complexities and organizational cultures that are driven by a flurry of technological advances, remote or hybrid work opportunities, and merger and acquisition activity. In turn, this has affected how professionals seek out mentoring relationships, as Higgins and Kram observe:

> Individuals will increasingly look beyond organizational boundaries for multiple sources of mentoring support as they navigate their careers. There will always be an important place both in research and in practice for traditional mentoring relationships, but our review of the career and mentoring literature suggests that this traditional model is but one configuration individuals may expect to experience in their careers.

The late Dr. Linda Phillips-Jones, the grandmother of mentoring research, derived from her study of hundreds of mentor-mentee partnerships that "mentoring is much more 'examinable' and more complex than first thought." In fact, in her strategy handbook-cum-assessment tool, *Skills for Successful Mentoring: Competencies of Outstanding Mentors and Mentees,* the psychologist and author finds that successful relationships in this vein demonstrate specific, identifiable proficiencies, processes, and behaviors that support learning and change. These interfaces further result in more effective mentee–mentor relationships.

Conversely, relationships that lack a structured process and specific skills leave a lot to be desired. Phillips-Jones argues that, mired in mediocrity, they provide ample breeding ground for frustration on the part of both participants. The seeming failure of these ill-begotten undertakings further reinforces the erroneous assumption that mentoring doesn't work.

A rich array of ingredients must be blended together for these relationships to bear fruit. The combination of sufficiently demonstrated skills, advanced and refined with frequency and consistency, increases the odds of sustaining a "mutually satisfying and productive" mentor–mentee experience.

Since mentoring has the potential for true personal, professional, organizational, and societal transformations, myths related to the nature, development, and cultivation of these bonds are detrimental to individuals' career trajectories and well-being, as well as to the workplaces that support them and that require each associate to bring their best each day.

The understanding of mentorship becomes increasingly muddied when we throw in two other closely related terms: **sponsorship** and **coaching**. We begin by exploring the notion of mentors and mentees because these are the partnerships that most readers will likely have the greatest familiarity with. Odds are, one has at least considered the prospect of mentoring or being mentored at some point (though the perception of what that relationship means may be built on a shaky foundation).

Fortunately, in my travels presenting on topics of developmental value to leaders around the world, the vast majority have engaged in mentorship. It is not uncommon for those individuals to have experiences that mirror my own. When polled informally by me, they enthusiastically agree with the following statement: "I have benefited greatly from mentors throughout my career."

My research has led me to define a **mentor** as

- an individual **who has knowledge** and **shares it with you** (the "mentee") and
- someone who **talks *to* you.**

A mentor is distinguished from a **sponsor**, who is characterized as

- an individual who **has power and influence** and will **use it *for* you** (the "sponsee");
- someone who **talks *about* you**;
- a "mentor-plus," hyperactivated as your champion or advocate; and
- an individual with access to the rooms that you aspire to be in and who actively advocates for you by sliding your name across the table to other powerful and influential people.

A **coach**, differentiated from either a mentor or sponsor with a unique set of characteristics, is defined as

- an individual **with expertise** who uses it **to teach or train you** (the "coachee");
- someone who **provides feedback, asks questions**, and **guides discovery**; and
- an expert who elevates your performance, transcending the developmental fundamentals and healthy foundation advanced by mentors and sponsors to drive performance.

From an outcome perspective, mentorship is *development* oriented, sponsorship is *advancement* oriented, and coaching is *performance* oriented.

Let's use these definitions as a baseline. They are an important facet of our conversation, as all discussions flow from these well-informed descriptions. We are not drawing conclusions based on hunches or on flawed, unfortunate, or anecdotal experiences within the restrictive confines of personal relationships. This baseline understanding of mentors, sponsors, and coaches is integral as one rounds out one's personal team or advisory board.

Dr. Ruth Gotian, an authority on mentorship and leadership development at Cornell University–affiliated Weill Cornell Medicine in New York City, points out that a **mentor** likely is an individual whom you already admire, respect, and aspire to be like. However, as differentiated from role models, a mentor presents a true partnership that may serve one in "a moment" or over the longer term, even throughout the duration of a career. Mentors (plural) can be a team of individuals who guide one's career and/or development as a person.

> A mentor enables you to revise and fine-tune your strategy, introduces you to people in their network, teaches you skills you should know, and provides emotional support when needed. They provide career and psychosocial support as you navigate the various triumphs and tribulations of your job. Mentors are generally volunteers.

The **sponsor** carries around a metaphorical spotlight, which they use to illuminate all of your hard work and achievements to their powerful network and circles of influence. Sponsors draw attention toward you when prestigious or "stretch" opportunities present themselves. These opportunities ultimately lead to career-defining and life-changing promotions. For example, the sponsor may shine a light on you when awards nominations are being solicited by an employer or industry group.

While the sponsor traditionally holds a senior role, this is not always the case. Peers can nominate each other for awards. Juniors can shine light on seniors' accomplishments. Likewise, one is not constrained to a limited number of avenues to spread the sponsee's name. Individuals may be "virtually" sponsored with "Attaboys!" or "Attagirls!" on social platforms, "in writing," or in person within the rooms that the sponsee aspires to. Regardless, sponsorship is not to be taken lightly by either the sponsor or the individual being sponsored. It is, after all, the sponsor's reputation on the line when throwing their full weight behind you. Think of this partnership as the beacon that lights your route to the sponsor's extended networks and all of the opportunities they represent.

In her copious published works, Gotian references others who have sought out her expertise on specific challenges or situations.

"People who come to me for coaching often do so to work on their leadership skills, overcome imposter syndrome, develop executive presence, and/or learn how to become the expert in the room," she writes. In these roles, she served as a **coach**. She defines coaching as a guiding hand to aid an individual in developing and enhancing specific skill sets within a clearly defined or finite time frame.

The "start" and the "end" of this type of relationship is dictated by the coachee and by their personal journey and progress. Coaches are further differentiated from mentors in that they are typically (though not always) compensated for coaching as a professional service. Organizations may offer in-house or outsourced coaching for C-suite leadership. Motivated individuals on the road to those high-level roles or who lack access to formal coaching within their workplaces may seek out private coaches, which Gotian calls a "worthy investment." Additionally, managers may switch into "coach" mode, offering feedback or helpful guidance to bolster skill development in the day-to-day processes of team interactions.

To these mentoring categories Gotian adds a fourth—**role models**, which she describes as "someone you look up to and respect," yet "you may never meet the person." That doesn't stop you from wanting to emulate their "executive presence," public speaking skills, or ways of connecting with others. You may draw inspiration from the role model's visibility within your organization, accomplishments, or professional brand. There is something about them that you can pinpoint as worthy of your admiration and respect.

How one invests one's time, heart, and even money is unique to the individual. Some readers may have identified that special person who fulfills all of these responsibilities and needs, at least at this particular moment. It's more likely, however, that there are multiple individuals who take on these defined roles to accelerate one's career, psychosocial health, and performance. That single individual's impact can have a ripple effect throughout an entire organization, community, industry, and beyond.

> Bidirectional:
>
> "Involving, moving, or taking place in two usually opposite directions."
>
> —Merriam-Webster

When interfacing with a variety of audiences, from early careerists to more experienced executives, I emphasize the importance of being mentored, sponsored, and coached. This truth extends to almost every step, chapter, or season of one's life, with the notable exception of sponsorship toward the end of a leader's career. (During the last few years of one's career, a sponsor may be rendered obsolete.)

If you were to sit in on one of my keynotes or lectures, you would get a resounding and enthusiastic "Always!" from me in response to the question, "When do we need mentors, sponsors, and coaches?" And while I have shared with many a professional the rich rewards that follow uninterrupted guidance on this front, there are certainly some phases (potentially driven by life events or workplace circumstances) that make mentors, sponsors, and coaches all the more important and enriching to your life.

Notably, **career transitions** may call for a sounding board, feedback, trusted counsel, advisement, and expertise. Any transition—be it moving into a new role, changing departments or organizations, or relocating to a geographical area far removed from the markets that represent one's roots or historical familiarity—may demand such perspective.

Additionally, times of **adversity** are ripe opportunities for us to pluck from the wisdom of those whom we trust. Consider the last time you were in a "downcycle." Light at the end of a dark tunnel may arrive courtesy of mentors, coaches, and other sounding boards who provide just the perspective and objective insights necessary to navigate a series of soul-sucking setbacks—everything from being passed over for promotions or receiving less-than-stellar performance reviews, to flat-out foibles or fumbles that can leave us reeling. One can come out of these situations armed with the guidance that lends itself to healthy persistence, resilience, and the courage to keep showing up.

What we perceive as defeats often end up being opportunities in disguise. The COVID-19 pandemic—a recent adversity all of us can relate to, especially within the healthcare field—has further demonstrated the need for authentic and meaningful connections. The pandemic fundamentally shifted our ability to devote time and intentionality toward nurturing our whole selves and building the connections that enable trust, psychological safety, and social well-being.

With so much ongoing chaos and uncertainty around every corner, it could be argued that leadership and mentoring sells itself as a valuable investment and tool in the current environment. Yet our ability to invest the time and dedication that these relationships deserve has never been more constrained.

There is also something to be said for seeking out wise counsel during the "good times." Congratulations, you're on a great tear! You are landing enviable, high-potential assignments and projects, and you're getting noticed for your exceptional achievements. When in an upcycle of **success**, honest self-reflection is a vital ally. Recall the factors that contributed to achieving these successes in the first place. Our industry has no dearth of talented role models. Just because you have enjoyed extended success that seems to have no end does not mean your personal and professional development should "sleep" or "go on holiday." It is critical to keep the momentum going.

Opportunities to connect, adapt, grow, and learn are more valuable in great times than almost any time. As our economic ebbs and flows continuously show us, the good times don't last forever. Plus, it is important to keep one's feet on earth—to ensure that hubris does not get in our way, preventing us from moving beyond our current level of growth and performance. Step back. Evaluate complacency. Nurture awareness of potential biases and blind spots that can present risks to our bright futures and career outlook. It can be difficult to candidly self-assess, and there are always insights to be gleaned from the perspective of others whom we look up to and whom we hold in high esteem.

MENTORSHIP: ESSENTIAL AT ALL STAGES

As a resource for curated career advancement content, the Ivy Exec indicates that resistance to mentoring may be loud and overly proud; for instance, readers may feel satisfied and articulate a common refrain: *I'm already where I want to be. Why do I need mentoring?* This statement certainly suggests a level of complacency. In the article "Mentorship Matters: The Career Benefits for Executive Professionals," the Ivy Exec points out,

> Are you ever truly done growing and learning? Mentors can help with career development, but the concept isn't solely about financial and position growth, it's about continually doing better at what you do, and thereby, growing and developing the people around you.

When an individual says they don't need mentoring because they're already where they want to "be," this statement calls for honesty, introspection, and substantial self-reflection. Yes, one's skill sets and technical aptitudes may be quite sound, but there are likely weaknesses or even niche talents that can be honed or taken to new heights.

By extending a gracious hand toward others, you garner new insights into fields you assume you have mastered or into areas of practice that you thought you knew better than yourself. Furthermore, you are exposed to roles, positions, fields, or areas of expertise that are outside your comfort zone. The power of perspective supports personal growth within respective employer organizations as well as insights into traits that may be applied when searching, recruiting, onboarding, or promoting talent within or outside the institution or company.

The gains associated with mentoring help one carve out an edge in the multitude of additional roles encountered while ascending the organizational ladder. The mentored are undoubtedly in more favorable positions to take on new responsibilities outside the functions originally honed with formal training and previous work.

Additionally, never underestimate **psychosocial needs**. My husband and I have intimate knowledge of this imperative. As our eldest child neared graduation from high school, we sought out the perspectives of a mentor couple whose children had already "flown the nest." Taking the long view, we wanted to be prepared for this significant parenting milestone. We've applied veteran empty-nesters' experiences and wisdom when navigating this transition. After all, they know best. They've walked the path! Let this be a reminder to all of us; golden nuggets of expertise and sage advice come in many different forms and cover considerable ground. How fortunate are we to benefit from their experience, lessons learned, and hard-earned expertise?

We all walk a variety of different paths in our lives, and not all are straight lines from cubicle to office to boardroom, or to the C-suite. Particularly in our personal lives, paths often diverge or end up looking less like lines on a map and more like incongruous tangents or messy webs. It is critical to think beyond the four walls of our organizations, workplace structures, and hierarchies. Seek input from those who have "been there, done that," regardless of where these experiential sources reside.

EMBRACING THE BIDIRECTIONALITY OF THE PRACTICE

The term *bidirectionality* recognizes that paths often go two ways. Just as we have benefited from being well mentored, well sponsored, and well coached, we must turn around, acknowledge, and invest in those behind us, around us, or passing by us. As leaders, be intentional in "catching" those passersby who may demonstrate promise but whose talents require nourishment and cultivation.

This call to action particularly resonates when identifying and nurturing the talents of individuals who are members of traditionally underrepresented groups or when engaging in strategic diversity, equity, and inclusion efforts. It is not adequate to assume that these relationships will emerge organically or spontaneously, especially among groups for whom there have traditionally been barriers to upward mobility within organizations and larger society. Hundreds of years of history fraught with subjugation and discrimination have taught us that such an approach is dangerously flawed and works only for the individuals at the top of the power structures.

It is particularly vital for healthcare professionals to be intentional in committing expertise and experience to others as mentors, sponsors, or coaches. There is limited time and brain space left over at the end of each day, given the onslaught of demands that are presented by our industry. So we must strategically invest, protect, and guard those precious moments by using them to develop others, provide feedback, advocate, and coach. Otherwise, there will always be "fires" that overtake our schedules. Boundaries must be established and protected, lest we miss out on transformative opportunities.

Within this same breath, it is important to consider that the modern mentoring relationship is built on mutual respect and is of mutual benefit. As platitudinous as it may sound, there is much for the mentor to learn from the mentee. In fact, this notion is also the basis for other types of mentorships that defy the conventional.

No longer should we limit our thinking on mentorship to the image of the older and more seasoned professional, paired with the younger and green-as-grass newbie, or of duos that tend to resemble each other (with the exception of the mentor having a few more gray hairs!).

Furthermore, these relationships have tended to be forced on us by formal initiatives or programs, which are hollow in that, too often, they simply represent yet another box for our employers to check off. There are almost certainly better ways to go about forging and sustaining successful relationships in the workplace and within our industry, and the large body of leadership development research bears this out.

At no time in our careers should we stop growing and investing in ourselves. This growth can come from the most surprising of places or sources, especially as we step back and lift up our organizations and industries by elevating others through service as mentors, sponsors, and coaches.

KEY TAKEAWAYS

- Mentoring has the potential to cause true personal, professional, organizational, and societal transformations.
- Mentors have knowledge and share it with you.
- Sponsors have power or influence and will use it for you.
- Coaches have expertise or perspective and use it to guide you to discovery.
- Mentorship is development oriented, sponsorship is advancement oriented, and coaching is performance oriented.
- Mentorship, sponsorship, and coaching are bidirectional.
- We always need mentorship, but especially in seasons of transition, in seasons of challenge or adversity, and in times of particular success.
- Investing in mentorship in both our personal and professional lives is important.

REFERENCES

Gotian, R. 2021. "Role Model, Mentor, Coach, or Sponsor—Which Do You Need?" *Psychology Today.* Published January 24. http:// psychologytoday.com/us/blog/optimizing-success/202101/role -model-mentor-coach-or-sponsor-which-do-you-need.

Higgins, M. C., and K. E. Kram. 2001. "Reconceptualizing Mentoring at Work: A Developmental Network Perspective." *The Academy of Management Review* 26 (2): 264–288.

Ivy Exec. 2021. "Mentorship Matters: The Career Benefits of Executive Professionals." Accessed October 1, 2022. http:// ivyexec.com/career-advice/2021/mentorship-matters-the-career -benefits-for-executive-professionals.

Phillips-Jones, L. 2003. *Skills for Successful Mentoring: Competencies of Outstanding Mentors and Mentees.* Grass Valley, CA: Coalition of Counseling Centers.

CHAPTER 2

The Business Case for Mentorship

THE CASE FOR mentorship in business is so solid that the Center for Creative Leadership (CCL), a global nonprofit leadership development network boasting more than 1 million alumni across 160 countries, has further developed and refined its white paper *Mentoring First-Time Managers: Proven Strategies HR Leaders Can Use.* This handbook of sorts is authored by two thought leaders in topics including organizational psychology, first-time management, cross-cultural leadership development, and strategic coaching and mentoring: William A. "Bill" Gentry, PhD, and Richard J. Walsh.

Gentry and Walsh took on the challenge of addressing an overlooked truth: **First-timers to formal leadership positions, those of the freshly minted promotion, arc often not equipped for the transition.** These individuals underestimate how tough the move into leadership will be. In fact, Gentry and Walsh note that in their work with organizations, the CCL often hears from business reps who assert that "these [first-time] leaders are not prepared," "they do not have a path forward," "they can't transition successfully," or "they're suffering."

Without appropriate development and support, Gentry and Walsh say, *everyone* suffers—managers, their teams, the broader organization, and (looking down the road), the "HR management pipeline." This cascade of negative effects, triggered by a poor leadership promotion or hire or a poorly prepared first-time manager (FTM), ultimately causes the organization's bottom line to suffer.

"First-time managers are an important part of an organization's talent and succession management," the authors state in their executive summary. "In turn, organizations may attempt to help first-time managers make the transition into leadership easier by implementing a formal mentoring program."

Such structured programs transcend the casual notion of mentoring, whereby one expects mentors and mentees to connect and grow their relationships organically. In this model, no strategic or intentional grooming takes place whatsoever. The relationships either achieve the connection and traction to propel them onward and upward, or the chemistry is simply not there and the relationship expires as naturally as it was brought (or matched) together.

The implications for the sustainability of one's talent—now and notably well into the future—are great.

Consider this:

- In a report for the Exit Planning Institute, the leading certifying body of exit planning and succession advisors, Christopher M. Snider notes that 50 percent of all business exits are characterized as a "forced exit."
- A "forced exit" means that owners and leadership are forced by influences beyond their control (and that were not addressed with appropriate planning) to leave their businesses on terms other than their own.
- The "forced" part comes about from an unexpected and unaccounted-for combination of the "Five Ds": death, disability, divorce, distress, and disagreement.

Mentoring and supporting key employees minimizes the risks of leaving one's organization or position under unfavorable circumstances. The organization as a whole is addressing the big topics that fall under the business succession umbrella, as it should, well before a slew of leaders retire or otherwise go through the exit door potentially because of some of those "Ds."

Furthermore, appropriately grooming individuals to manage others optimally goes a long way toward minimizing or eliminating distress and disagreement. It is natural, even healthy, to have some disagreement or pushback. An active discourse and diversity of thought should be encouraged. In fact, these are hallmarks of psychologically safe organizations and workplaces; however, depending on the nature of the disagreement and how long it has been allowed to simmer, there may be some sources of tension that are insurmountable and stem from long-term problems associated with poor management. Fortunately, these tension triggers can be headed off.

Citing the Committee for Economic Development's Conference Board, the *Mentoring First-Time Managers* report notes that CEOs were most challenged on the human-capital front to improve those managers who specifically fall under the "frontline and first-time" category. Why is there such considerable opportunity within this segment of the worker population?

- While they may not be the most visible population within one's organization, *first-time or frontline managers make up the largest population of leaders within businesses.*
- Furthermore, many of these frontline managers *are managing others for the first time* in their careers.
- In addition to making up the biggest percentage of leaders in the workplace, these frontline managers are tasked with *directly leading the most workers* within the workforce.
- Frontline managers *set the tone for pipeline-building efforts* well into the future. So what you do now in hiring and onboarding these individuals can either propel the organization forward or hold it back. Remember that each leadership position generally begets another leader behind it.
- Similarly, these managers are the "bench strength." They are supposed to be the leaders whom you can call upon

within your organization and whom you can pull from the sidelines. Ideally, they effortlessly fill those roles when the stars of the organization leave for greener pastures, have to step away for a time, are promoted elsewhere, take on new gigs, or encounter whatever life has in store for them.

- Likewise, bench strength is critical to one's organization during times that are frequently described as "wars" for optimal talent. You want these managers to present a seamless transition into positions that are affected by critical talent and skill shortages. You do not want your bench filled with underskilled people who do not inspire confidence or instill respect, or who are lacking other qualities—such as "heart"—that are necessary in the best leaders.

As stated by Gentry and Walsh, many of the inadequately prepared first-timers on the frontlines *do* have the self-awareness or sense of self to know that they are failing. These individuals acknowledge and articulate feelings of helplessness:

Even though the trend to focus on frontline managers can ultimately become a competitive advantage for your organization, **most first-time managers (FTMs) on the frontlines are not ready to lead, receive limited if any development, and believe they are failing at their jobs.** [emphasis in original]

Furthermore, research has confirmed what FTMs sense and what the CCL is concluding here. Gentry and Walsh go on to cite a Careerbuilder.com survey, which reported that

- almost six of every 10 new managers (58 percent) have received no formal training at all related to development or managing people before transitioning into their first-time management position;

- two of every 10 FTMs are doing a poor job, according to their subordinates; and
- more than a quarter (26 percent) of FTMs surveyed said they were "not ready to lead others."

Manchester International, by way of the CCL, also asked the question, "Why are so many new managers and executives failing?" Over the course of their research, the firm found that a staggering 40 percent of those managers failed within 18 months of being promoted.

When one considers the amount of effort and money that is traditionally spent on onboarding and transitioning, the results are even more concerning; however, time and time again, these findings suggest either misplaced resources or a failure on the part of the employer to provide sufficient or appropriate resources to managers who are leading for the first time.

This research is further substantiated by Bersin & Associates (now Bersin by Deloitte), a talent management consulting provider. In the *Leadership Development Factbook 2012*, analysts Karen O'Leonard and Laci Loew looked at first-level, frontline supervisors' readiness for their respective positions. Many of these supervisors are also FTMs. They found that these leaders "receive the least amount of money and support in training and development dollars compared to all other managerial populations (e.g., mid- or senior-level executives)."

Additionally, the CCL's internal researchers discovered that half of all managers in organizations were regarded as "incompetent, disappointments, the wrong hires, or failures." The researchers conclude, "Clearly, more should be done to help FTMs make that all-important transition from individual contributor into a leadership position as smoothly and effectively as possible."

It bears repeating that, since these FTMs manage most of the people within their respective organizations, they can then have the greatest influence over key areas of performance and sustainability, ranging from client (patient) satisfaction to employee productivity, engagement, and psychosocial well-being.

As today's boomers are in close proximity to (or halfway out) the exit door, it is an absolute must that ready and capable successors are prepared to take over for them. Formalized leadership or mentoring should also be in place, as this feature has been noted as lacking in large bodies of research literature.

"Formalized mentoring," as used throughout this book, largely refers to officially supporting and sanctioning leadership development and mentor-mentee relationships. Formalization further suggests structures, policies, clear and specific support, and guidelines set forth by the organization to aid in launching, successfully positioning, and nurturing these relationships over the longer term.

"Informal mentoring" refers to relationships that are launched, maintained, and ended by those involved within the relationship: the mentor or the mentee. These relationships arise organically or spontaneously. And while it can be said that too often mentoring has been left to the "fingers crossed, we hope this works!" approach, there are cases where Gentry and Walsh conclude that these organically hewn partnerships can be just as beneficial for FTMs as partnerships built within formal frameworks.

The CCL suggests a combination of both approaches; after all, who would turn away a great mentor or mentee opportunity if it landed in one's lap? It is just as important to refrain from waiting for those relationships to emerge or come to us. Organizations quite literally cannot afford to take a wait-and-see approach.

Regardless of how these relationships are developed and deployed, Gentry and Walsh emphasize that access to allies or mentors in the workplace fosters

- better preparation for promotions,
- higher success rates,
- greater satisfaction with jobs and careers,
- higher ratings on performances measures or indicators,
- innovation and creativity,
- greater resiliency to setbacks, and
- stronger networks.

In a meta-analysis of more than 15,000 articles published between 1985 and 2006, researchers in the *Journal of Vocational Behavior* confirmed the results and, in turn, the importance of mentoring relationships. These findings feature outcomes in six key areas:

- Behavioral
- Attitudinal
- Health-related
- Relational
- Motivational
- Career

The longitudinal research indicates that mentoring drives outcomes in each area, and these various categories inform and feed into each other. For instance, the partnerships that are fostered beget relational outcomes, which set a motivational foundation that further drives positive career, behavioral, attitudinal, and health-related transformations. The study concludes the following:

> Mentoring is significantly correlated in a favorable direction with a wide range of protégé outcomes.

STATE OF THE WORKPLACE

Around one-third of the more than 100 million people in America who work full time are engaged and inspired at work, according to Gallup's *State of the American Workplace: Employee Engagement Insights* report, derived from a massive, multiyear engagement survey of employees. So what exactly are the other two-thirds of employees doing?

Millions of workers (about 16 percent) are the exact opposite of "engaged"; they are "actively disengaged." These employees are, as the report puts it, "miserable in the workplace and destroy what the most engaged employees build." They are not merely unhappy. They are acting out on their personal misery. Their unhappiness is being used as a missile, to actively undermine colleagues' healthy performance and engagement every day. The remaining half of American full-time employees fall into neither category: they are "not engaged," but they're not "actively disengaged," either.

The report says that the remaining 51 percent of workers "are not engaged and haven't been for quite some time." If we all haven't been them, we have seen them—they're the "zombies" at the watercooler. They are not actively spreading malcontent. They're going through the motions, punching the time card, doing the bare minimum. They *exist*, but that's about it.

An earlier version of the Gallup report from 2013 was quick to implicate "bosses from hell" in the epidemic of the actively disengaged. Gallup chairman and CEO Jim Clifton noted that these bosses "make [workers] miserable." Then there are the hordes of the not-engaged who are sleepwalking through the job: "not inspired by their work or their managers."

There are substantial, real dollars on the line when teams are not managed well. Naturally, Gallup has put numbers to the effects of poor managers on team performance and well-being. The top 25 percent of best-managed teams experience *70 percent fewer* on-the-job accidents compared to their "worst-managed" counterparts in the bottom 25 percent of teams.

Additionally, poorly managed team members have recorded 40 percent more quality control defects than their counterparts with stellar managers. The poorly managed teams are also incurring far greater healthcare costs. These teams' members are more likely to visit your institution's emergency room or occupational health service.

Gallup calculates that the total costs attributed to active disengagement and so-called "managers from hell" is a whopping *$450 billion to $550 billion each year*. In the 2013 report, Clifton concludes:

Having too few engaged employees means our workplaces are less safe, employees have more quality defects, and disengagement—which results from terrible managers—is driving up the country's healthcare costs.

According to Clifton, for too long business schools have failed to instill in leaders a critical truth, the single biggest decision that they will make in their jobs, dwarfing all of the rest: *whom you name manager*. "When you name the wrong person manager," he continues, "nothing fixes that bad decision. Not compensation, not benefits—nothing."

Now, imagine the impact that doubling the number of great managers can have on our economy and society. You can effectively double the number of actively engaged employees alongside their confidence- and inspiration-boosting leaders. It is the millions of engaged employees who truly drive positive organization-wide and economy-wide changes, including

- groundbreaking innovations,
- new clients,
- brand ambassadors,
- an entrepreneurial culture,
- renewed energy and morale, and
- sustained boosts to the bottom line.

MENTORING THE RIGHT MANAGERS

So what exactly does fostering great managers have to do with conversations around mentorship, sponsorship, and coaching?

In the Gallup survey, the business case was made for selecting the right managers and establishing strong connections with each and every employee. An organization with a culture of mentorship prioritizes the identification of each employee's strengths and matches that talent to positions where those strengths are best leveraged.

Smart leaders and organizations make substantial investments (time, talent, treasure) toward helping associates better know themselves so they can rise to their unique exceptionalism. Then, these leaders double down to facilitate those authentic connections and access to allies, which further aid the maximization of employees' distinctive strengths.

Notably, researchers emphasize that attention must be paid to aligning the young or early would-be leader's strengths to their responsibilities. Not everyone has the "it" factor to be an excellent leader or manager, and the statistics bear this out. As Gallup notes, a number of suboptimal managers lead by example and perpetuate more of the same in their followers and teams, time and time again. It's a vicious circle.

To transform engagement and thereby the workplace, there must be the following intentional strategies:

- "Scientifically" selecting managers for their *specific talents and strengths related to managing people.* Management positions should not be treated as promotional prizes, where you just "put in the time" and the manager title will come to you. Instead, managers must be selected from the get-go to be successful in the specific functions and demands that will be placed on them. They must truly be "management material," with the right combination of abilities to support, empathize with, and position others to their greatest potential each and every day and to empower and engage the team members that report to them.

  Of course, this concept flies in the face of the "Peter principle." Back in the 1960s, the Canadian educator and organizational structure researcher (or self-proclaimed "hierarchiologist") Dr. Laurence Johnston Peter surmised that individuals within a hierarchy tend to rise to "a level of respective incompetence." As Jonathan Grudin puts it in "The Rise of Incompetence," employees are continually being promoted because of their successes in previous jobs—that is, until they reach levels at which they are no longer competent. The skills at their now-high position do not necessarily reflect the skills they exercised and performed so adeptly in the past. Their experience, knowledge, and strengths simply fall short of the demands and responsibilities placed on them in this higher role.

The employee will not qualify for another promotion after reaching the ominous-sounding "Final Placement" or "Peter's Plateau." They are stuck. And if you get enough of those "stuck" or "plateaued" managers, you really have a dark situation on your hands. Each wildly incompetent and dissatisfied manager can further infect their staff. If you have ever been perplexed by a sudden Jekyll-Hyde transformation in a top-performing employee following that employee's promotion, you may be witnessing the Peter principle in action. The Peter principle is often used to explain the shortcomings of organizations and why organizations with increasingly experienced people (who are further rewarded for their tenure and strong track records) appear to regress rather than move forward.

- *Cultivate well-selected and well-prepared managers* who are truly management material. There should be a system or structure in place to successfully onboard new managers into these roles. It is critical to provide ongoing support to these individuals, establishing clear goals for engagement. Hold managers accountable to those priorities. Get quantitative by tracking and measuring the progress that has been made. You must know what the manager is doing, as only then can improvements in the areas of management effectiveness, employee engagement, and workplace well-being be made.

This process relies on intentionality—identifying specific objectives, and following up by measuring and tracking where someone is in terms of achieving those goals. These characteristics get to the very essence of the accountability that has been sorely missing because of our societal and organizational histories, as well as our damaging tendency to let managers and the managerial promotion process go on autopilot.

- The beating heart of any organization should be its *people-to-people connections.* The previous item in this list discusses connecting with new or would-be managers in meaningful ways, with outcomes that include a level of accountability. This approach drives performance and positive outcomes in both intangible and tangible ways. In establishing a culture whereby managers are properly supported and mentored, sponsored, and coached, each manager is also better equipped to turn around and bidirectionally support their team members or direct reports.

There is intimate familiarity with establishing and maintaining the connections that foster better employee relations, customer and stakeholder relations, and overall monetary returns on an organization's investment in its talent- and engagement-building. It is important to maintain an awareness that each interaction with the manager's staff has the potential to either hinder or help one's perspective on day-to-day work responsibilities and functions, and the workplace as a whole.

KEY TAKEAWAYS

- Mentorship is particularly important for first-time and frontline leaders.
- Investing in mentoring leaders at all levels of the organization builds bench strength and contributes positively to succession-planning efforts.

- Mentoring leads to desirable workplace outcomes, including better preparation for promotions, higher success rates, greater job and career satisfaction, higher performance ratings, greater innovation and creativity, greater resiliency to setbacks, and stronger networks.
- Leaders and organizations that invest in building awareness of strengths drive both performance and engagement within individuals and teams. Leaders are the primary key to unlocking performance and engagement in teams and organizations.
- Leaders who actively mentor, sponsor, and coach produce powerful outcomes in and through their people.

REFERENCES

Eby, L. T., T. D. Allen, S. C. Evans, T. Ng, and D. DuBois. 2008. "Does Mentoring Matter? A Multidisciplinary Meta-Analysis Comparing Mentored and Non-mentored Individuals." *Journal of Vocational Behavior* 72 (2): 254–267.

Gallup, Inc. 2017. *State of the American Workplace: Employee Engagement Insights for U.S. Business Leaders.* Published February. http://gallup.com/workplace/238085/state-american-workplace-report-2017.aspx.

———. 2013. *State of the American Workplace: Employee Engagement Insights for U.S. Business Leaders.* Published June. http://shrm.org/ResourcesAndTools/hr-topics/employee-relations/Documents/Gallup-2013-State-of-the-American-Workplace-Report.pdf.

Gentry, W., and R. Walsh. 2015. "Mentoring First-Time Managers: Proven Strategies HR Leaders Can Use." Center for Creative Leadership. https://doi.org/10.35613/ccl.2015.2047.

Grudin, J. 2016. "The Rise of Incompetence." ACM Interactions. Published January. http://interactions.acm.org/archive/view /january-february-2016/the-rise-of-incompetence.

O'Leonard, K., and L. Lowe. 2012. *Leadership Development Factbook 2012: Benchmarks and Trends in U.S. Leadership Development*. Oakland, CA: Bersin & Associates.

Snider, C. M. 2019. *The State of Owner Readiness: 2019 Nebraska Report*. Westlake, OH: Exit Planning Institute.

CHAPTER 3

Supporting Diversity, Equity, and Inclusion

REPRESENTATION AND MENTORING, sponsorship, and coaching (MSC) go hand in hand. For leaders to be successful and effective, a "champion," or rather a *network* of champions, is not merely a "nice thing to have." It is a *must-have*. This truth is no more pronounced than when we are speaking about championing—mentoring, sponsoring, coaching and generally lifting and elevating—on behalf of populations across our organizations and broader society that have historically been underrepresented.

Awareness of, and strategic efforts to address, the marginalization of so many are increasingly on organizations' and leaders' collective radars. Tremendous social justice awareness brought on by transformative global crises have played a defining role in pushing these efforts and priorities out of the shadows and onto center stage. Yet this does not change the fact that underrepresented groups *simply are not present enough* in our leadership circles, boardrooms, and elsewhere—where important decisions are being made, power is being wielded, and influence is exuded.

For many, the lack of access to leaders that "look like them," and the comparative disparities between those who have traditionally held positions of power and everyone else, raises a few eyebrows. Advocates of influence are needed. The great "RBG" (the late Supreme

Court Justice Ruth Bader Ginsburg) perhaps put it best: "If you're going to change things, you have to be with the people who hold the levers."

This is not a discussion to further put on the defensive those white males who have conventionally been present in all of the rooms and sectors that matter. There must be some linking of arms to address persistent challenges. Mere awareness and dialogue are inadequate. *Real action* must take place. It starts with conversations, resources, infrastructure, and support. But, again, that is just the start.

- In its Global Gender Gap Report from 2018, the World Economic Forum notes that "women outnumber men in almost every educational level" and that they account for at least half of the total workforce in most of the nearly 150 countries surveyed. Yet participation and educational attainment are not translating into positions of power and leadership; the global financial and advisory firm Grant Thornton says that as recently as 2018, women filled just 24 percent of senior manager roles.
- The disparity is even more pronounced when analyzing the CEOs who head up the largest corporations in the United States. A mere 8.2 percent of CEOs at Fortune 500 companies are women, according to updated figures released by the Women Business Collaborative (WBC) in its October 2021 report. While this figure is a move in the right direction, up from 6.6 percent and 3 percent in 2019 and 2018, respectively, the WBC, which is made up of 59 women's business organizations, asserts that "progress is still too slow and not reflective of the nation."
- Women of color fare even worse when it comes to representation in the C-suite. Broadening their evaluation from the top 500 US companies to the top 1,000 companies stateside, the WBC reports that only 1 percent of CEO positions across Fortune 1000 companies are held by "multicultural women."

- In healthcare, representation at the highest levels of executive leadership and governance is no better. According to a study published by Jason Mose in *Women's Health* Report, although women compose more than 80 percent of the healthcare workforce, they hold only 13 percent of CEO roles in health systems and only 27 percent of hospital CEO roles. Another study published by McKinsey & Company found that when accounting for all C-suite roles in healthcare, 59 percent are held by white men, 11 percent by men of color, 25 percent by white women, and 5 percent by women of color.

When one considers the real benefits that are secured as a business by developing leaders who better reflect our society and by making strides toward parity, the disconnect between these returns and the lack of investment and seeming acceptance of the status quo is even more perplexing.

There are decades of expert research in this field:

- According to global nonprofit Catalyst, the Fortune 500 companies with the greatest percentage of women serving on their boards of directors significantly financially outperformed, on average, the companies with the lowest female representation on their boards.
- Companies with the highest women's representation, Catalyst noted, outperformed in the "return on equity" category by upwards of 53 percent; similarly stronger-than-average performance was seen with "return on sales" and "return on invested capital," with average outsized performance on those fronts at 42 percent and 66 percent, respectively.
- In her article "The Business Benefits of Gender Diversity," Dr. Sangeeta Bharadwaj Badal, formerly of Gallup, reports that "gender-diverse" business units (of the 800-plus units studied within two retail and hospitality companies) also

experienced outsized financial outcomes as compared to teams unequivocally dominated by one gender *or the other.*

That last point is emphasized because the findings did not conclude that one gender was "better" than the other or that gender contributed so favorably to exceptional performance. Rather, it was noted that "men and women have different viewpoints, ideas, and market insights, which enables better problem solving." Badal continues that "gender diversity is vital to any workplace. Not just because it's a laudable goal; it simply makes bottom-line business sense."

Badal offers as proof survey findings that quantitatively demonstrate qualitative "hunches": hiring a demographically diverse workforce can result in real financial gains. Within the retail company, Gallup found that the diverse units had, on average, 14 percent higher revenue than less diverse business units (5.24 percent versus 4.58 percent). The hospitality company's demographically diverse business units secured a 19 percent higher-than-average quarterly net profit than business units that left a lot to be desired on the gender diversity front ($16,296 versus $13,702).

When diverse female-male representation was combined with high levels of engagement, financial performance absolutely soared, with a dramatic 46 percent increase in revenue and 58 percent higher net profit among those within diverse and engaged units in retail and hospitality, respectively, as compared to their less diverse and less engaged counterparts. As Badal puts it, "These results show the additive effect of gender diversity and engagement on a company's bottom line."

Having a larger percentage of women within an organization's workforce resulted in many of the same expansive, far-reaching benefits associated with the ripple effect of connecting one's day-to-day work life to one's sense of purpose, self-awareness, and strengths. In the article "Women in the Workplace: Why Women Make Great Leaders and How to Retain Them," the Leading Effectively staff at the Center for Creative Leadership (CCL) noted that the percentage of women within businesses serves as a predictor of greater job satisfaction, higher levels of employee engagement, and decreased rates of burnout for all workers, regardless of gender, age, ethnicity, or leadership level. In short, having more women in the workplace is associated with positive outcomes for women *and* men.

Leading Effectively's findings demonstrate how women leaders and colleagues were *more favorably rated by men*. The authors highlight this: "Specifically, men reported being more satisfied with their job, enjoying their work more, and not feeling as burned out if they worked for companies that employed higher percentages of women."

CNN Business's Matt Egan looked at CNNMoney analysis and Catalyst research findings, which substantiated both the lack of a talent pipeline for female CEOs as well as the effect these CEOs have on a company's wealth. Egan reported that "having leaders with diverse experiences and backgrounds often translates to financial success. That's largely due to the fact that women bring different skills than men and that can lead to more thoughtful deliberations about risk-taking and appealing to female consumers." His article quotes former Frontier Communications CEO Maggie Wilderotter, who states that women are "very good at multitasking, having a sixth sense with people, are nurturing and service-oriented."

The CCL pointedly suggests supporting women's ability to advance in their careers in another article titled, appropriately, "Women Need a Network of Champions." Organizations should ensure that they are maximizing all talent, regardless of gender or color, and prioritizing "sponsoring and mentoring for women—particularly by influential leaders, who are often men."

The CCL dubs mentorship and sponsorship a key strategy for professional advancement, performance, and success, saying that "both mentors and sponsors are critical to helping aspiring women leaders gain the perspective and connections they need to take on larger roles and advance their careers." In fact, as we will explore more extensively later, an extreme shortage of opportunities for sponsorship has persisted. Women tend to describe themselves as being "over-mentored to death," whereas an imbalance in sponsorship exists between men and women.

You'll recall that sponsors are the "advocates" or "allies" in the workplace world. They're the ones that talk *about* you rather than talking *to* you. There is considerable power behind their access to other influential people and to the rooms that are inaccessible, especially in your earlier career stages. Sponsors serve as connectors, making the introductions and getting your name out so that when opportunities arise to stretch your skills and to really show up, your name is at the fore.

In an article in the *Harvard Business Review*, the London Business School's Herminia Ibarra states, "Too few women are reaching the top of their organizations, and a big reason is that they are not getting the high-stakes assignments that are prerequisite for a shot at the C-suite."

Why is there a dearth of coveted "high-stakes" assignments? Ibarra attributes this shortfall to a frequent "lack of powerful sponsors demanding and ensuring that they [women] get these stepping-stone jobs." Some companies have halted formal sponsorship programs. They have reportedly cited pushback from execs who felt they were being asked to advocate for someone whom they didn't know well or didn't think was "ready" for the assignment. This isn't a good reason, Ibarra contends, to give up on the notion of sponsorship.

Rather, she sees opportunities for organizations to reinvent how these relationships are approached. Ibarra recommends, in part, that companies shift away from sponsors as "either/or" and shift toward sponsorship on a spectrum, different behaviors that are flexible enough within this model to allow for varied types of commitment. Thus, there is breathing room within mentorship, sponsorship, and coaching relational structures to effectively connect women and other underrepresented demographics with powerful difference-makers and opportunities.

DISPARITIES IN REPRESENTATION

As Stefanie K. Johnson and David R. Hekman remark in the *Harvard Business Review*, myriad factors are at work that ultimately have led to a situation in which 85 percent of corporate executives and board members generally look the same: white men, often "of a certain age"! Johnson and Hekman observe that, on its face, this "suggests that white men are continuing to select and promote other white men."

In "Women Need a Network of Champions," the CCL points out how people tend to, by nature, gravitate toward others who look like them:

> Male leaders may unconsciously be inclined to mentor and champion other men. Similarly, women may not feel comfortable asking somebody several levels up—especially someone who doesn't look like them—for advice or sponsorship. So even with no other factors at play, more men than women are sponsored, and leadership power structures remain largely unchanged.

Johnson and Hekman echo this sentiment. They say women's representation at the executive and board levels "hasn't budged for decades" and that the aforementioned in-group bias of favoring and promoting those from "like" groups reinforces stereotypes and inequality. These inherent inequities, certainly not built in a day, are problematic for the talent pipeline and present barriers to two important strategic priorities for executives: succession planning and preparing the next generation of talent within organizations.

At the time of Matt Egan's analysis for CNN Business in 2015, only 14.2 percent of the top five leadership positions at the companies in the S&P 500 were held by women, while the total number of female CEOs at these companies was a paltry 24. In fact, it's such an issue that when a woman at the top of an eminent company makes any sort of move, it can be front-page news for weeks on end.

And any time a woman exits that position or moves on from the corporate world to, say, academia, it is shouted from the rooftops: *We have lost yet another one!*

While all CEO moves within top companies merit such attention, women get outsized attention because there are so few of them. They are, indeed, like the elusive snow leopard or white buffalo in the wild. They should certainly not be this much of a rarity. In conjunction with the release of a flurry of analyses by Catalyst and others on female C-suite leadership in 2015, Rita McGrath—a Columbia Business School Professor, author, and speaker—was quoted by Egan as follows: "It's kind of shocking, really. With all of the attention the issue gets, you'd think companies would be doing better."

Egan's analysis further found that only 16.5 percent of the four positions directly beneath the CEO in S&P 500 companies were held by women. So there remains a shallow pool of leaders to pluck from for the next generation of female CEO talent. McGrath states simply, "If you don't have women in the pipeline, they are not going to get the top job."

Partially constrained by generalizations that tend to peg all members of a certain group, whether women or men, as having the same personality traits or behavioral tendencies, Egan's analytics further highlighted another vital facet: the lack of women in so-called "mission-critical jobs." These positions are critical for the organization's success and serve the dual function of grooming future leaders.

A deeper dive into the analysis found that many successful women ended up in human resources and investor-relations roles. While these positions were still important, Egan notes that these jobs "don't serve as a gateway to the top of the C-suite."

In fact, this notion can be reduced to a game of sorts. Go to an organization's "meet the team" page. Guess where the women are? In all likelihood, if any women serve in executive roles, those roles function in some way within a customer-relations capacity. Women are often chief talent officers or chief brand officers or, in a more recent phenomenon, chief diversity, equity, and inclusion officers. What they are often *not* is chief financial officer (CFO), chief operating officer (COO), or chief information officer (CIO). In healthcare, this imbalance is on full display. Jason Mose notes that women fill only 27 percent of hospital CEO roles, 39 percent of COO roles, 35 percent of CFO roles, and 28 percent of CIO roles, while they represent 73 percent of all chief human resources officers and 91 percent of all chief nursing officers.

Real efforts to embark upon and sustain relationships in varied MSC forms can extend historically underrepresented populations' capabilities and further stretch us beyond the stereotypes of what top leaders look like within our organizations and communities. Real *action*, not just *attention*, on this front is the right thing to do. We need to think beyond pure bottom-line motivations.

> In order to achieve true diversity, equity, and inclusion in our organizations and reap the benefits that result from it, the time has come for executives to invest in both developing and advancing well-qualified future leaders of all walks of life, backgrounds, and origins from within their ranks.

KEY TAKEAWAYS

- Representation and mentorship, sponsorship, and coaching go hand in hand.
- Research confirms disparities in representation at the highest levels of leadership and governance and compensation within healthcare and throughout various sectors.
- Diversity at all levels of leadership and in the boardroom drive demonstrable and desirable organizational outcomes.

- Mentorship and sponsorship are key strategies for advancing gender equity and achieving parity.
- Research confirms that women fail to be selected for visible, high-stakes assignments that are requisite for achieving senior executive roles.
- Savvy organizations can rethink the way they nurture talent and take intentional steps to enhance diversity among those whom they develop and advance through mentorship and sponsorship initiatives.
- Mentorship, sponsorship, and coaching can move the needle on the important business outcome of diversity, equity, and inclusion.

REFERENCES

Badal, S. 2014. "The Business Benefits of Gender Diversity." Gallup. Published January 20. http://gallup.com/workplace/236543/business-benefits-gender-diversity.aspx.

Berlin, G., L. Darino, R. Groh, and P. Kumar. 2020. "Women in Healthcare: Moving from the Front Lines to the Top Rung." McKinsey & Company. Published August 25. https://www.mckinsey.com/industries/healthcare-systems-and-services/our-insights/women-in-healthcare-moving-from-the-front-lines-to-the-top-rung.

Catalyst. 2007. "The Bottom Line: Corporate Performance and Women's Representation on Boards." Catalyst. Published September 14. http://catalyst.org/wp-content/uploads/2019/01/The_Bottom_Line_Corporate_Performance_and_Womens_Representation_on_Boards.pdf.

Egan, M. 2015. "Still Missing: Female Business Leaders." CNN Business. Published March 24. http://money.cnn.com/2015/03/24/investing/female-ceo-pipeline-leadership.

Grant Thornton. 2018. "Women in Business: Beyond Policy to Progress." Published March 5. http://grantthornton.global /globalassets/1.-member-firms/global/insights/women-in -business/grant-thornton-women-in-business-2018-report.pdf.

Ibarra, H. 2019. "A Lack of Sponsorship Is Keeping Women from Advancing into Leadership." *Harvard Business Review*. Published August 19. http://hbr.org/2019/08/a-lack-of-sponsorship-is -keeping-women-from-advancing-into-leadership.

Johnson, S. K., and D. R. Hekman. 2016. "Women and Minorities Are Penalized for Promoting Diversity." *Harvard Business Review*. Published March 23. http://hbr.org/2016/03/women -and-minorities-are-penalized-for-promoting-diversity.

Leading Effectively staff. 2022a. "Women in the Workplace: Why Women Make Great Leaders and How to Retain Them." Center for Creative Leadership. Published December 2. http://ccl.org /articles/leading-effectively-articles/7-reasons-want-women -workplace/.

———. 2022b. "Women Need a Network of Champions." Center for Creative Leadership. Published March 30. http://ccl .org/articles/leading-effectively-articles/why-women-need -a-network-of-champions.

Mose, J. N. 2021. "Representation of Women in Top Executive Positions in General Medical-Surgical Hospitals in the United States." *Women's Health Reports* 2(1): 124–132.

Women Business Collaborative (WBC). 2021. *Women CEOs in America*. Published October 13. http://www .ascendleadershipfoundation.org/research/2021-women-ceo -in-america-report.

World Economic Forum. 2018. *Global Gender Gap Report 2018*. Published December 17. http://weforum.org/reports/the-global -gender-gap-report-2018

CHAPTER 4

Fostering Well-Being

> Well-being: "The state of being happy, healthy, and prosperous" (Merriam-Webster).

In leadership and life alike, very little is done in isolation. For every action, there is a reaction. Mentoring, sponsorship, and coaching demonstrate this interconnectivity. We live, work, and play within communities. In every sphere, we collaborate with others. And leadership is a "people" business—*relational*, not *transactional*. Furthermore, the consequences of such relationships build upon each other, with one benefit begetting another. As we'll explore, the well-being that is supported by MSC begets numerous other positives, from an unshakeable sense of self and purpose to good physical health—having the energy and stamina to lead the fullest, richest life possible.

Because of its connection with an abundance of work opportunities that allow leaders to focus on their personal strengths and with the decline in active disengagement across workforces, this concept could lend itself to its own book. In fact, Gallup developed a proprietary well-being index in conjunction with the digital health and wellness company Healthways (which was acquired by Sharecare in 2016).

Since it was launched in 2008, the well-being index has surveyed more than 4 million US adults at a rate of 10,000 respondents, aged 18 and older, on a monthly basis. This index is a great complement to the work that internal and external researchers have completed in relation to the links among awareness of one's own strengths, the ability to practice and refine those strengths on a consistent basis, one's overall happiness on the job, capacity to motivate and inspire others, and productivity. Of course, the satisfaction that one feels at the workplace also strongly influences the satisfaction that one feels in all spheres of one's life.

The index has its finger on the pulse of five "essential elements" to well-being and the important characteristic of resiliency:

1. **Purpose**—You really love what you do. You feel motivated to achieve your goals.
2. **Social**—You have a support system, healthy relationships, and loved ones.
3. **Financial**—Economic "management" promotes reduced stress and increased security.
4. **Community**—You feel safe and love where you live, and have a strong sense of pride in the neighborhoods that surround you.
5. **Physical**—You have the health and energy to get things done and to lead life to the fullest.

According to Sharecare's most recent Well-Being Index reporting from 2021, the "purpose" category of the index actually improved from 2019 measurements, up to 64.7 from 59.0. The importance of a sense of purpose is significant, as it is directly related to performance and motivation. When we like what we do or find meaning and gratification in our work, we're much more likely to achieve excellence and overcome hardships or challenges that are inherent in the workplace. Furthermore, this report shows that purpose is directly linked to greater emotional resilience and a decreased likelihood of developing chronic health conditions. In states where residents experience higher levels of purpose well-being, they also experience 1.4 times lower rates of clinical depression, 1.5 times lower rates of heart attacks, 1.6 times lower rates of coronary artery disease, nearly 2 times lower rates of chronic obstructive pulmonary disease, and 2.1 times lower rates of chronic kidney disease.

You'll recall that professionals who are empowered to use their strengths were noted in the workforce engagement data to be far less likely to be disengaged and hostile in their work environments. The Sharecare well-being index further substantiates these findings and the role that truly satisfying, strengths-based, supportive work plays in workplace health and overall societal health; it reports that individuals who are thriving in four of the five elements are also engaged at work.

The connection continues between well-being categories and another matter of high importance to organizations: employee retention. According to Sharecare, there is an inverse relationship between well-being and resignation rates. States that reported lower financial and community well-being ratings reported higher rates of employee resignations. For leaders and organizations, the message is clear. Prioritize and invest in well-being, and lead by example in bolstering it.

Businesses with sincere aims and smart investments designed to heighten their talent's development, engagement, health, and well-being are furthermore less likely to grapple with

- costly, frequent, and regressive **turnover**,
- frequent or severe **accidents on the job**,
- **costs** associated with workers' compensation insurance and return-to-work initiatives following injuries,
- frequent and costly **thefts** of workplace and worker property, and
- **quality incidents** that erode customer trust and satisfaction.

It follows that workgroups who are thriving on the job and outside the workplace also have considerably higher *customer* engagement, as well as comparatively favorable productivity and profitability.

Historically, there has been a tendency to underestimate the power and worth of "soft skills" within the workplace. Skills such as the ability to communicate clearly with others or to negotiate and empathize with colleagues have been minimized in favor of a hard-nosed, "just the facts, ma'am" style of leadership.

However, the mere presence of well-being indices and research demonstrates that the tides are turning. And the facts provide a groundswell of quantifiable insights into the effect that acknowledging these so-called "soft skills" in our leaders—and further developing and refining them through mentors and other forms of support—has on the bottom line.

Daniel Goleman's seminal article "What Makes a Leader?" offers supporting research for the Carnegie Institute of Technology's assertion that technical knowledge accounts for only 15 percent of one's financial success. As for the remaining balance (85 percent) of that success? It comes down to the characteristics dismissed through the decades by workplaces: personality, communication, negotiation, and leadership. Taken together, we may call these characteristics "emotional intelligence." In his book *Emotional Intelligence*, Goleman puts it like this:

> Effective leaders are alike in one crucial way: They all have a high degree of what has come to be known as emotional intelligence. It's not that IQ and technical skills are irrelevant. They do matter, but mainly as threshold capabilities; that is, they are entry-level requirements for executive positions. But my research, along with other recent studies, clearly shows that emotional intelligence is the *sine qua non* of leadership.

Sine qua non. The essential condition. The absolute must or necessity. And guess what? The carving out or refining of this "must-have" ultimately comes down to the organization and its approach to developing these skills. Technical aptitude, as noted, is the baseline. To move from good to great involves other skill sets. This is also the difference that is made by enlisting new forms of support, such as coaching, as one matures or evolves in his or her career to take performance to the next level.

Purpose is fundamental to both engagement and well-being. In fact, that sense of "why you do what you do" has been characterized as one of the most important predictors of well-being by Dr. Richard J. Davidson, a neuroscientist and founder/director of the Center for Healthy Minds at the University of Wisconsin–Madison.

"People with a strong sense of purpose . . . tend to have better physical health, more quality relationships and even improved brain function," Davidson remarks via the center's article "Four Ways to Cultivate Purpose." In one study highlighted by the center, older people with a low sense of purpose were more than twice as likely to die in the next five years as people with a strong sense of purpose. The center highlights "purpose" as "among the most robust psychological predictors of mortality."

The center also takes a big swipe at the illusion that high income equates to happiness. It points to research among almost 100,000 people across 94 countries, which examined the links between satisfaction with life and satisfaction with income. The results indicated that "people with a stronger sense of purpose were less likely to judge their lives based on how much money they made, and were also more satisfied with how much money they already had."

This type of research informed actionable items designed to make the notion of purpose in life a "personal and lived reality." Many of these action items align well with discourse on intentional programs and cultural development around strengths-based mentoring and guidance.

As mentors, we can guide others from putting motivating forces and values "in writing" to reflecting on and reframing how day-to-day situations (especially challenges) can be resolved, addressed, or overcome through the lens of purpose and what we hold dearest to us.

Rather than getting caught up in solving all of the world's problems, we find that simple shifts in perspective, gleaned *from* mentors or even *as* mentors, can be invaluable when leading by example. Opening our eyes and ears to expanded circles around us can spur actions that are driven by purpose and that further reinforce the connections between one's values and higher purpose. As Davidson puts it, one is always in control of one's perspective: "Even the most challenging situations in life can become deeply meaningful."

Purpose was certainly identified right off the top as an essential element of Sharecare's Community Well-Being Index. The dots have been connected among a strong sense of purpose, satisfaction with one's overall life, better physical health, improved relationships, keen cognitive function, and overall longevity—again, many of the essentials as measured by the index.

WEAVING WORK AND EVERYDAY LIFE TOGETHER

The average worker will spend 90,000 hours of their life at work. Put another way, that's one-third of an individual's lifespan! It is small wonder, then, that work has such an impact on the rest of our lives. Our happiness, or our disdain, for the nature of our work and/or our workplaces can easily spill over into our personal, familial, and social realms. This is even more the case for those in the healthcare field, whose hours clocked in a lifetime will no doubt far exceed the average noted by Gettysburg College in an article about industrial-organizational scientists at the RAND Corporation, who evaluated individuals' lifetime investment in work.

Increasingly, work "spillover" into the rest of our lives has been facilitated by those pesky devices that allow us to always be "on" and connected. Another absolute: we must be motivated with a strong, positive purpose and ensure that we as leaders and organizations provide the opportunities and meaningful connections for people to rise in the positions that are best suited to them. In doing so, we also lift those who are most affected by the properly mentored, sponsored, and coached leader—be it the leader's direct reports, customers, and patients or their family members, friends, and peers.

We and the organizations that employ and surround us must focus on advancing the notion of purpose, acknowledging its importance, and clarifying what that purpose means to each individual. This resolution requires some intentionality and care, taking time for us to step back, pause, and reflect. So much flows from purpose and other essential ingredients behind thriving well-being; how we act on this purpose can either enhance or hinder the quality of our talent, our workforce performance, and the reputation of our brand to would-be talent, leaders, and our target constituencies and stakeholders.

The struggles that are inherent within the healthcare universe are unquestionable and have only been underscored to others outside of our world as global crises have presented themselves. The following words from author Jon Gordon (*The Seed: Finding Purpose and Happiness in Life and Work*) will no doubt resonate with many of you: **"We don't get burned out because of what we do. We get burned out because we forget why we do it."**

Research clearly and regularly substantiates the positive role that other people have on our well-being. Things (personal possessions) play a far inferior role in the five essential areas of holistic wellness, despite their increasingly ready availability to us in day-to-day life.

The late, great Jim Rohn (a grandfather of motivational speaking who mentored the likes of Tony Robbins and Jack "Chicken Soup for the Soul" Canfield), is also widely recognized for coining the "Rule of Five" theory, which hearkens back to the importance of scrutinizing the company that one keeps. It is an extension of the law of averages whereby Rohn theorized that if one does something often enough, a ratio results and this ratio is perpetuated. One may think about this in terms of reaching out to 10 different representatives or organizations to build strategic community alliances with an affiliated institution. If only one of those organizations decides to join forces with you, precedent for this ratio has been set and will likely continue unabated. The 1:10 ratio will be sustained as the long-term average.

Acknowledging that this is a small sample size, even seemingly statistically insignificant scenarios are quite telling and establish a basic Rohn-ism: One should become accustomed to patterns once they have been set. There is something to be said for the power of "practice makes perfect," but once these averages or ratios are established, they take on a life of their own and are hard to shake because of the hold they have on our overall mindset. The strategic leader is always mindful of the company they keep, the impact that company has, and the path upon which it places them.

The law's implication for a "people practice" (mentoring) is substantive. Rohn is widely credited with saying, "You are the average of the five people you spend the most time with." This "Rule of Five," also widely attributed to Rohn, suggests that each element of well-being is influenced and shaped by the five individuals closest to us. These personal or professional figures have a significant impact on our behaviors, habits, and patterns as well as the performance and trajectories of our careers and our family and social lives. We tend to become like these individuals. There is as much potential for our "Five" to elevate us, to perpetuate a plateau, or to bring us down with them. It very much depends on the mindsets, tendencies, trajectories, and behaviors of those who then support and sustain any personal changes, as this shortlist of close relationships casts an oversized shadow on your todays and tomorrows.

Consider the high school graduate who leaves their "nest" for the first significant amount of time. In college, they are sharing close quarters with a range of individuals who are potentially from far-off communities and who may have completely different cultural backgrounds, lifestyles, and socioeconomic circumstances that also shape their personality attributes and proclivities.

The changes in these college-aged students are marked and occur in a matter of weeks or months. By the time they return home for the holidays, their families may think they are reuniting with a new person. The high school student they knew is no more. That individual now has new dietary preferences and sleep habits, speaks and behaves in markedly different ways, and exhibits notably changed interests.

This same tendency to absorb others' energies and inclinations continues as we mature beyond college, well into our adult lives. There are certainly times when it can be life altering or even lifesaving to step back and reflect on our "Five": Do the individuals whom we surround ourselves with the most play it fast and loose with their health, safety, and overall well-being? Or are they conscientious about doing the right things when it comes to respecting their bodies—as well as their emotional, mental, and spiritual selves—by consistently nurturing those spheres with exercise, a nutritious diet, and mentally stimulating activities? Do we find ourselves always engaging with folks who tend to "live in the moment" and impulsively indulge in extravagancies all under the "instant gratification" banner? Or do we gravitate toward the investors, savers, and practical types who are mindful of the future when spending and consuming in the present?

Your parents were right—who you "hang with" matters. The implications and stakes only grow higher as we age and have more responsibilities and people who count on us—be it our families, friends who are "like family," or cherished workmates and workplace teams. With so much on the line, we must distinguish between those who enrich our lives with their inherent differences in lifestyles, values, and goals and those whose differences are potentially damaging, can set our careers and overall wellness back, or lull us into a pattern of stagnation or mediocrity.

KEY TAKEAWAYS

- Mentorship, sponsorship, and coaching all contribute directly to well-being outcomes in both individuals and organizations.
- Overall well-being comprises different categories or elements: purpose, social, financial, community, and physical.

- Well-being drives performance and engagement in the workplace and overall societal health, and it reduces negative outcomes such as turnover, accidents on the job, theft, and quality incidents.
- Emotional intelligence is essential to leadership excellence.
- Purpose is fundamental to both engagement and well-being and is confirmed to contribute to better physical health, higher-quality relationships, and even improved brain function.
- Clarity of purpose is often honed and refined in relationship with mentors and coaches, leading to valuable outcomes in life and in leadership.
- The company that you keep will have an impact on the person you become. Curate your circle intentionally.

REFERENCES

Center for Healthy Minds. 2022. "Four Ways to Cultivate Purpose." Accessed October 5. http://centerhealthyminds.org/join-the-movement/four-ways-to-cultivate-purpose.

Gettysburg College. 2017. "One Third of Your Life Is Spent at Work." Published January 17. https://www.gettysburg.edu/news/stories?id=79db7b34-630c-4f49-ad32-4ab9ea48e72b&pageTitle=One+third+of+your+life+is+spent+at+work.

Goleman, D. 2004. "What Makes a Leader?" *Harvard Business Review*. Published January. https://hbr.org/2004/01/what-makes-a-leader.

———. 2005. *Emotional Intelligence: Why It Can Matter More Than IQ*, 10th-anniversary ed. New York: Random House.

Gordon, J. 2017. "Know Your Why: What is Your Purpose?" Published July 10. http://jongordon.com/positivetip/know-your -why.html.

Sharecare. 2022. *Sharecare Community Well-Being Index: 2021 State Rankings Report.* Published July 13. https://wellbeingindex .sharecare.com/wp-content/uploads/2022/07/Sharecare -Community-Well-Being-Index-2021-state-rankings-report.pdf.

CHAPTER 5

Types of Mentors

JUST AS LEADERS do not all look a certain way, there is energizing freedom in knowing that not all mentor relationships look, feel, or function in the same way. This truth is particularly freeing for the busy healthcare executive: to know that there are numerous avenues and methods for sharing one's expertise and experience, whether by setting an example as a leader for up-and-comers or working within the confines of the more conventional master–apprentice and teacher–student relationship.

In fact, broadening our perspective and definition of mentorship gets to the very heart of what these efforts aim to do in the first place—to propel us forward as professionals and leaders. In doing so, as the individual advances, early-stage leaders and their direct reports follow suit. Improved teams inform improved organizations. The communities in which we work, play, and live are also buoyed by support systems that transcend stiffly defined settings.

Similarly, to engage and lift everyone means extending a handshake beyond our offices, neighborhoods, industries, and social circles. It is only then that true progress is made in terms of diversity, equity, and inclusion.

When considering mentorship, I challenge you to think more holistically about ways that you can experience this practice. Here are a few examples:

- Traditional mentorship
- Peer mentorship
- Reverse mentorship
- Mentorship constellations
- Mentors of the moment
- Formal mentor relationships
- Informal mentor relationships

The **traditional mentorship** model is probably what first comes to most individuals' minds when the word "mentor" is uttered. These are the allies who are typically your senior and are more experienced in life or leadership. They've "been there, done that" and can teach or train you from their learnings. These individuals may have been your role models before they were your mentors. Perhaps you aspire to be like them "when you grow up." As seasoned professionals who double as mentors and role models to look up to and emulate, they behave as allies; they command respect by their very presence.

While these individuals are typically incredibly busy, they prioritize and intentionally set aside the time to invest in sharing their wisdom. They are seasoned from years or decades of experience and the hardest of hard knocks. They are not stingy in sharing what they have learned—in some cases the hard way—so you don't have to repeat their mistakes. There will be plenty of opportunities to learn through other missteps! They take a genuine interest in you, and maybe even see a bit of themselves when they were younger (or earlier into their careers) in you.

While individuals within these traditional relationships have historically been saddled with stodgy or stuffy master–apprentice-style relationship constraints and formalities, the most authentic and successful relationships can be more more relaxed. There is freedom to "be," and only when there is trust and psychological safety between both parties can the relationship bear fruit. What this means is that achieving the comfort level to laugh, have fun, bare your soul, and not always answer, "Fine" to the question "How are you doing?"

This is the type of vulnerability that we as a society crave so much, but it must be nurtured and protected.

By its very nature, the **peer mentorship** model is not weighed down with the heaviness of decades of expectations, narrow definitions, and stifling constraints. This basic characteristic brings with it tremendous freedom and the ability to take a big breath and relax. The pressure of being "perfect" and impressing someone you look up to isn't heavy on your shoulders. This is an incredibly freeing proposition.

With that said, such peer relationships were not characterized as "true mentorship experiences" in earlier-generation mentor research. After all, those who fall within a relatively similar age range, friend group beyond the workplace, position, or "rank" could never lead you to meaningful growth, could they? Oh, my friend, they can and they do!

Don't overlook the value of cultivating relationships with like-minded peers. As I mentioned in the last chapter and will expand on in chapter 8, the power of colleagues who challenge, pace, encourage, and exhort you cannot be overstated.

Because of pesky competitive dynamics among peers at the same level of advancement and with similar career pursuits, ambitious professionals might be missing out by failing to tap into the expertise that surrounds them and that may be accompanied by a built-in or established level of trust and natural enthusiasm to be vulnerable. Peer groups are often close to us, but we can sometimes hold them at a distance in terms of their perspective and counsel being properly leveraged for professional and personal development.

As an underused resource, peers as individuals with unique insights and experiences to offer may be considered on their own personal merits. Some peers may have strengths that lend themselves well to a particular challenge or project that you are working on, whereas for the next phase you may desire or require the expertise of a peer with a completely different background, personality, and set of characteristics and talents.

As puzzling as the peer mentor experience may be to the scholar examining and shaping mentoring at the dawn of structured relationships, the notion of **reverse mentoring** is similarly mind blowing. If peers have conventionally not been acknowledged or properly engaged within these mentoring models, then what could a junior-level colleague, even a subordinate or early-careerist, have to offer?

For starters, it is integral that we break free of the hubris that stands in the way of continuous improvement and our drive to reach new levels of performance and developmental progress. As the "Father of Sports Medicine," the late Dr. Jack Hughston had a name for this phenomenon of arguably too much comfort with ourselves and our place in the hierarchy. and too little acknowledgment that life passes us by as we stand haughtily on our comfortable perches. He liked to characterize it in the following manner:

> When you're green, you're growin'. When you're ripe, you're next to rotten.

Hughston thrived by these words—and it showed! The orthopedist lived well into his eighties and was almost 50 years old when he became what he wanted to be when he grew up by focusing his practice primarily on sports medicine and sports-related injuries.

The eponymous Hughston Sports Medicine Hospital represents the first facility of its kind in the United States. "Visionary," "ahead of his time," and "pioneer" are terms used time and time again to describe Hughston's never-ending innovation, growth, and advancement. Hughston was not content with sitting at the top of his game in orthopedics. Instead, he ended up advancing medicine and healthcare designed to treat athletes of all ages and stages and reached across disciplines in sustaining health and elevating sports performance.

Magical things can happen when we stop believing at a certain vaunted season of life that we know everything and instead acknowledge that inspiration and insights can come from untraditional, if not unlikely, places.

In reverse mentoring, the "traditional mentor type" (the seasoned, senior professional or executive) trades places with the "green-as-grass" junior-level newcomer, the "traditional mentee type." The mentor may get schooled in how to effectively and efficiently use technologies and social platforms. Or they broadly garner invaluable, fresh perspective from the up-and-coming generation. One's high perch in an organization is not always synonymous with an expansive, 360-degree view. Sometimes when we are that high up in our organization, the clouds can obscure our view of the collective that is below us for now but is quickly asserting itself as our organizations' and communities' futures.

It takes conscientious, intentional effort to put our feet back on the ground and provide us with practical, in-the-trenches perspective. It is increasingly accepted that the most successful mentor-mentee partnerships are those that are mutually beneficial. There is a great deal of satisfaction for the typical mentee to have the tables turned, to swap traditional roles and enlighten the senior mentor.

Likewise, there are tremendous benefits to be had for mentors who step back and give of their time, talents, and even treasures in some cases (if, for instance, we are talking about lucrative training or career-development opportunities for mentees or other up-and-comers under our wings). Anyone who knows me also knows that I am fond of the Walt Whitman quote that so aptly conveys the value that comes from mentoring: "The gift is to the giver, and comes back most to him—it cannot fail."

In the end, maintaining the status quo is often not the laziest way of doing things; on the contrary, it is a time-consuming, unnecessarily exhausting, and dangerously regressive attitude. This notion of "tradition for tradition's sake" is akin to cavemen pulling a massive box of boulders with sheer, manual, physical force. When approached by their forward-thinking counterparts, armed with humanity's first wheels, they don't rejoice and marvel at these more astute cavemen. Instead, those early traditionalists remark, "No thanks! We are too busy." Then they get back to pulling their box of rocks instead of using the world's first set of wheels. Don't be a caveman and reinvent the wheel. Picking up perspectives throughout our careers, including from those generations that are distant from us in chronological age, cultivates innovative, progressive, efficient, and transformative thinking and encourages the actions to put those boundary-shattering concepts into practice.

Mentorship constellations is an apt phrase to describe collaborative approaches to mentoring that draw in many perspectives and that are not limited to or dependent on one individual or partner. As with the groups of stars in the sky, a bigger picture comes into view when many beacons of expertise and experience are drawn together. Just as the stars in a constellation form recognizable patterns, shapes, and forms, our networks are able to lead each other and light the path toward individual and collective excellence and growth. Together, we weave brilliant, illuminating webs. By coalescing, we are able to shine brighter as a unit, rather than as one singular "star" within our organization trying to make our way. Put another way, enlisting a single mentor is less career enhancing than building robust networks or constellations of mentors, allies, and advocates.

In fact, these networks and constellations have been highlighted as important by thought leaders on the subject of mentorship, allyship, and development—Drs. Ruth Gotian, W. Brad Johnson, and David Smith. They identify networks as pivotal components of cultures that embrace and foster mentorship in more than mere messaging and performative gestures. For such organizations, mentorship is embedded into their very fabric and DNA. The existence of developmental networks is very much the thread that sews this change-agent culture together.

As Gotian puts it in "How to Develop a Mentoring Team" for *Forbes*, a single mentor is "limiting." A personal mentoring team puts you, the mentored, in the driver's seat. Characterized as "collective" with your "best interests at heart," this team shines with a "diversity of thoughts, perspectives, skills, and social capital." The greater the diversity of one's team, the greater one's potential and reach.

In a 2019 article for the science journal *Nature,* Gotian also describes how "indispensable" her personal advisory board has been since she first established this collective of reliable and clear-eyed thinkers a quarter of a century ago. These advisors paid off pretty much from the get-go; for instance, Gotian takes us back to 1996 and the onslaught of responsibilities competing for her attention when she was first embarking on a new role in managing a MD–PhD program at a sizeable US Ivy League medical school.

"Armed with the requisite education, relevant experience and a strong sense of tenacity," she recalls, "I thought I was up for the task." After 11 months of juggling daily duties (student affairs, budgets, crisis management, fellowship applications) with "special projects" (expansive interview days for applicants and competitive grant submittals), she remained undeterred:

> I felt I was capable of doing it at all—but I wasn't cognizant of what I didn't know. And I felt like I was constantly putting out fires. I was navigating through unwritten rules and unforeseen challenges, such as trying to find opportunities for the program and its students. . . . The to-do list was endless, and I always had countless balls in the air.

Sound familiar? One "harrowing" year later, Gotian turned to a source of advisement: a colleague at another school who had been doing the same type of work for *decades* instead of months. They reconnected in person during a conference, during which Gotian maximized her colleague's fountain of knowledge by peppering her with endless questions about admissions, alumni tracking, recruiting, and staying up to date on data collection for coveted National Institutes of Health training grants.

Notably, the colleague ended up revealing things Gotian never considered—from resources for finding alumni to the names of prominent faculty and administrators whom she needed to know. The duo then joined other conference participants, and the fledgling advisory panel matured and fluxed from there. "My success, capacity for clear thinking and sanity would have been greatly compromised were it not for this group," Gotian says.

As with many leaders, Gotian's has been a career journey blanketed with unending challenges, resources that should always be at her fingertips, and priorities that must be on her radar. Before long, Gotian was putting bidirectionality into action, organizing the conference that started it all, and offering her own valuable contributions within advisory team settings. Recruiting processes got a shot in the arm. Successful summer academic programming was launched, and methods for tracking and reengaging alumni were reimagined.

"Advisory team members have become a source of boundless information, co-presenters at conferences and good friends," Gotian remarks.

MENTORS OF THE MOMENT

Anecdotally, I illustrate to would-be and firmly established healthcare leaders alike the importance of breaking free from the confines of a single mentor within a relationship characterized by very narrow and specific features. Instead, one must view these engagements through the lens of **mentors of the moment**. These are individuals you can draw from at different moments, milestones, or phases within one's life and career.

More pointedly, it's important to consider that such a mentor (let's call him "Bob") is a fine advisor to draft to your team. He is, after all, a rich supply of technical knowledge and experience that can be gained only through trial and error; he may be the best source of counsel or wisdom at specific windows or steps within one's career. It is not an affront to realize that Bob's expertise or perspective may not be relevant or needed as circumstances change or as you advance up the ladder or reach across the table. Instead, another mentor's specific skill sets or advisement may be better suited to your new (or "of the moment") situation.

Having a sounding board or "kitchen cabinet" to call forth and seek guidance from as you traverse the career journey (from individual contributor to influencing force) is very much the embodiment of the truer, holistic definition of mentorship as a practice. It no doubt resonates with many readers, this professional evolution or progression in healthcare, whereby technical competencies hold an outsized importance at the outset of our careers—whether we are technically competent as clinicians, strategists, financial or operations wizards, or population health and informatics savants.

As we ascend in leadership, behavioral competency begins to assert itself as of greater importance. These competencies are tied less to IQ and more to emotional intelligence ("EQ") and include the practice of active listening and the use of our understanding of our unique strengths and weaknesses for the good of the whole. This level of self-awareness goes far when deferring to others, facilitating the most productive dialogues to achieve the most favorable outcomes, and empowering others within our organizations. Likewise, we must have the wisdom and humility to "own" what we don't know. Part of being a great leader is delegating and deferring to those who know best. You then celebrate and let others rise to their awe-inspiring potential, too.

As we rise to new heights of leadership, we must also reflect on how we allocate and value our precious time. Consider this: It is certainly more the norm than the exception to say yes to pretty much everything early into our careers. It is only natural to do so; we need to absorb as much knowledge as possible, and actually "doing" is superior to reading or approaching our day-to-day responsibilities from a theoretical perspective.

In many respects, among those just embarking on their career journeys, there is little choice involved. It is a must to build and refine one's technical competencies with the experiential. So this approach early on is not simply limited to the most ambitious, leadership-seeking colleagues among us. With the passage of time and the accrual of knowledge and experience, we have the freedom and, furthermore, the authority to say no every once in a while.

Now, *knowing* what is in one's best interests and actually *acting* on and verbalizing it are two very different things.

But how are "green" team members supposed to nourish their technical know-how if we as more seasoned professionals do not get out of the way? To be the most effective leaders (friends, parents, caregivers, community-builders, connectors), we must give ourselves some time and space for priorities that require our utmost attention and care. In this manner, we free up the best of ourselves—our energy and precious minutes on the clock—for the most mission-critical areas of our organizations and lives.

As we advance, there is also the increasing challenge of getting objective and meaningful feedback. There may be fewer and fewer individuals who are willing to "tell it like it is" as we gain tenure and further establish ourselves as authorities and role models in our fields.

An authority in executive-level leadership coaching, Dr. Marshall Goldsmith, has devoted an entire book to this concept of actively seeking new practices and "not the usual suspects" sources of unfiltered feedback and counsel to drive wise choices as one levels up. *What Got You Here Won't Get You There* is a title that speaks volumes about much of the content within; Goldsmith argues that the correlation between our behaviors and our success through the years is not causative. Sometimes, successful outcomes in our careers occur *in spite of* how we may have behaved through our career stages.

There is a natural human tendency to overestimate our abilities and organizational contributions and to underestimate the blind spots and weaknesses that are present even among the best of us. Comparably, there is no guarantee that the proclivities and activities that got you to your current, senior level will get you to the next level. Goldsmith speaks very much to the heart of mentoring, sponsoring, and coaching—this giving of one's self and the knowledge that can only be accrued by actual doing—when he writes, "Successful people become great leaders when they learn to shift the focus from themselves to others."

Varied advisory roles, while not defined models of mentorship, can occur in traditional hierarchical settings as well as in more relaxed, no-pressure settings. With that being said, stereotypes and strategies intertwined with mentoring relationships tend to lean heavily to one side or the other. The reality is, we need both **formal mentor relationships** and **informal mentor relationships** to flourish.

Indeed, by looking broadly at mentorship as more than a single person or relationship, we start to pull in varied voices and perspectives. Quite naturally, the structure and nature of some of these partnerships may be more traditional or formal, whereas other mentor-mentee partnerships may represent more fluid dynamics and far less rigidity in how partners interact and relationships evolve. By tapping into the relationships around us or those that are ripe for the picking, this effort lends itself to equally diverse and varied structures that feed our myriad needs and multidimensional selves.

PICKING YOUR TEAM

Ruth Gotian lends her considerable wisdom on this front to guide the "global thinking" that leads to a smart, well-assembled team of advisors. She encouraged us all to curate our board from diverse industries and geographies. Such diversity informs renewed thinking and new approaches to solving old problems.

Additionally, the team should not look like you; aim instead for a cross-section of genders, identities, ethnicities, generations, and even industries. *You* are the common denominator, while the team itself can ebb and flow as challenges and opportunities shift from one moment to the next. This approach to team building is demystified, courtesy of five actionable steps provided by Gotian's *Forbes* article:

1. **Name that goal!** Put some thought into immediate, attainable goals. Longer-term goals no longer seem like such a climb when you establish a near-term objective to pave the way. The path is then laid out before you—you just need to walk it!

2. **Clarify next steps.** It is critical to brainstorm and articulate specific milestones within the path ahead. This stage is where mentor teams can step in to help actualize the plan by providing insights to propel one forward and by connecting the advisee to other people who can support progress. The process of pulling these disparate voices together may be viewed as a bull's-eye, with three concentric circles.

3. **Establish the "inner circle."** Ask yourself: "Whom do I know best?" This intimate, most trusted of groups may be made up of spouses, partners, family members, close friends, and colleagues. You can count on these individuals to speak the unvarnished truth, even when it hurts the most. They know the "you" that others don't see behind the curtain—an understanding that must be built with the passage of time.

4. **Firm up the "middle."** As you work your way outward from the target, these relationships are no less important; they are just different. It is these differences that are vital to our personal and professional successes.

   This unique combination of intimacy and "arm's length" distance within the middle circle comes courtesy of our closest work colleagues. These individuals may not know your innermost secrets, but they have seen you rise from crises. They are largely folks with whom you are well acquainted, but you don't consistently engage with them. For instance, the colleague from your institution or a peer within your local community or charitable pursuit is well respected for their counsel on certain topics, yet you retain a less intimate and more infrequent relationship.

   Seeking out counsel on specific topics is important, because these middle-circle types boast niche knowledge that is beneficial to your growth and development. Summarily, these individuals are well aligned with your values and interests. They are aware of your tenacity, vision, and resiliency. In all likelihood, they know the raw, not-photoshopped "professional you" better than you do because of the power of objectivity. And there is a healthy level of reciprocity, in that these middle circle–ites contribute value to your journey, which then flows back the other way toward your personal advisors. They see your unique strengths and skills, and they benefit from the novel insights that you provide.

5. **Mind the "outer circle."** Because of the nature of the relationships in this circle and the sheer number of potential opportunities for partnering, it is often the most intense and challenging to define; however, the advisors in this circle can provide surprisingly satisfying personal and professional discoveries that ultimately lead to progress and advancement. Some of these individuals may be acquaintances within the industry or your area of specialty, whereas others are drawn from fields and industries outside your own. Ideal team members are leaders or experts whom you admire and who possess skill sets that are disparate from your own.

Consider adding to your list of "potentials" those former mentors whose skills and competencies have proven beneficial time and time again and with whom you have started to lose touch. Leverage opportunities to reconnect and build on already established relationships or to reengage and rebuild those valued and meaningful relationships that may be lost when life gets in the way. Likewise, when you assess yourself, your needs, and your opportunities for growth, former fellow trainees or classmates may rise to the surface as being the right match with the expertise and perspective that you need.

Lastly, consider the membership organizations you are most actively engaged with and the members whose talents would close your knowledge gaps. While communications with these individuals may be far more infrequent than others on your board, they know you well enough to carve the time out to respond to requests from you to pick their brain or "pick up where we left off."

It pays to have a broad spectrum of talents within one's board. According to Herminia Ibarra, there may be the **mentor** for advisement, support, and coaching; the **strategizer** whose inside-baseball advances defined blueprints from the conceptual to the actual; the **connector** who makes introductions on your behalf to influential others; the **opportunity-giver** providing career-defining, highly visible assignments and responsibilities; and the **advocate** publicly fighting for you in settings and rooms that are beyond your current reach. Regardless of industry, the skill of negotiating is always helpful, especially when linking arms across so many disciplines and fields. Cherish the diplomats of the world.

Gotian indicates that the low-hanging fruit when assembling these circles consists of the innermost confidantes who know the "personal you." Work outward from the bull's-eye, leaning into individuals who know the "professional you," and then take on the headier task of enlisting and building a multidimensional outer circle.

As with mentors of the moment, goals and plans are realized with the understanding that advisors surface and fade away. They may potentially emerge again or dim completely from your circles. A natural progression may occur that moves one's outer-circle inhabitants into the middle circle with time, partnering, mutual respect, trust, and reciprocal confidence.

Likewise, circle members may arise organically or within formalized network structures. As needed, leverage existing members to pull in additional people with much-needed skills, perspectives, backgrounds, and experiences. With a simple ask, team members lead to other invaluable advisors. *You* don't stand still; your *circles* must not remain static.

THE VIRTUOUS CYCLE OF MENTORSHIP

It is not surprising that many of the attributes we admire or seek to emulate are the same talents, skills, and perspectives that are exhibited by the most trusted advisors within our support team.

Mentors are sources of appropriate encouragement and validation, having been on the receiving end of the same within their own advisory-team relationships. They can be counted on for sound counsel, wisdom, expertise, and objectivity, as they've lived these characteristics from the "best." They know how to be comrades, putting their own pride and fierce competitiveness on the shelf. They know when and how to challenge, push, and pace because they have been challenged, pushed, and paced in the past.

Mentors deliver "light-bulb moments," whereby the confident mentee or advisee may get a reality check when struck by considerations that were never even on their radar. They, too, have realized, "I didn't know what I didn't know." Just as your advisors unlock your potential, they have had the keys to do so passed on to them from members of their personal boards of directors. Mentorship presents a cycle, with us as leaders having the opportunity to experience so many different roles and opportunities throughout our lives—the very roles that allow us to lead our fullest and richest professional and personal lives in the service and support of others.

KEY TAKEAWAYS

- Think more holistically about the types of mentor relationships that exist:
  - Traditional mentors
  - Peer mentors
  - Reverse mentors
  - Mentorship constellations
  - Mentors of the moment

- – Formal mentor relationships
- – Informal mentor relationships
- The practice of mentoring is an "output," but it can often have the paradoxical reality of giving back to the giver.
- Prioritize diversity when assembling the mentors you surround yourself with—diversity of thoughts, perspectives, skills, and social capital.
- As we ascend in leadership, behavioral competency begins to assert itself and present outsized importance compared to technical competency. Both are vital. Adapting throughout the journey is what sets outstanding leaders apart.
- As we advance in our careers, it can be increasingly challenging to acquire objective feedback. There may be fewer and fewer individuals who are willing to "tell it like it is."

REFERENCES

Goldsmith, M. 2022. "Coaching for Behavioral Change." Marshall-Goldsmith.com. Accessed October 1. http://marshallgoldsmith.com/articles/coaching-for-behavioral-change-2.

Gotian, R. 2020. "How to Develop a Mentoring Team." *Forbes*. Published July 6. http://forbes.com/sites/ruthgotian/2020/07/06/how-to-cultivate-a-mentoring-team-in-five-easy-steps.

———. 2019. "Why You Need a Support Team." *Nature*. Published March 27. https://www.nature.com/articles/d41586-019-00992-3.

Orthopedics Today staff. 2009. "The Hughston Clinic's Sports Medicine Focus Led to World-Class Orthopedic Center." *Orthopedics Today*. Published March. http://healio.com/news/orthopedics/20120325/the-hughston-clinic-s-sports-medicine-focus-led-to-world-class-orthopedic-center.

CHAPTER 6

The Value of Sponsorship

WRITING FOR *THE Muse*, author Jo Miller reinforces that having a mentor isn't enough anymore. "Don't get me wrong—mentors are wonderful," she continues. "They help you gain critical skills, navigate you through challenges at work, and offer a sounding board when you're at a crossroads in your career." However, she contends that a sponsor is necessary in addition to a mentor for those who wish to advance significantly in a competitive environment.

> Mentors help you "skill up," whereas sponsors help you *move* up.
>
> —Jo Miller

Miller's statement above draws a key distinction between mentors and sponsors. She likens the presence of a sponsor to a safety net, allowing one to confidently take risks, such as asking for promotions or stretch assignments.

"They provide a protective bubble and can shield you from organizational change like reorganizations or layoffs," she adds. "And they bring your name up in those high-level talent development discussions that take place behind closed doors. If your career is moving forward, chances are there's a sponsor behind the scenes, pulling strings on your behalf."

Marissa D. King, an organizational behavior professor at Yale University, echoes many of these themes in her article "How Finding a Mentor—or Even Better, a Sponsor—Can Accelerate Your Career." King also explores the idea that sponsors are willing to put their weight next to the sponsee's performance. Whereas mentors may be closer to friends than other MSC relationships, sponsors are more like investors. As King puts it:

> Their support is public and they use their reputation to support yours. Sponsorship is one of the strongest predictors of promotions and salaries—roughly equivalent to the number of hours someone works—according to a study that examined the careers of tens of thousands of employees and dozens of predictors of job success. For promotion prospects, sponsorship matters more than someone's gender, personality, education, and experience.

ACTIVATING THE "MENTOR PLUS" RELATIONSHIP

In chapter 1's introduction to the concepts of mentoring, coaching, and sponsoring, we defined sponsors as those individuals who talk *about* you, as distinct from mentors who talk *to* you. The sponsor-sponsee relationship is more about the (usually senior) leader exercising power and influence to be your champion in those "rooms" that are filled with equally influential and powerful people.

The Center for Creative Leadership (CCL) ("Women Need a Network of Champions") defines at greater length the nuances in roles, goals, and drivers behind the relationship, and associated actions between mentor and sponsor relationships.

By the time most leaders are halfway through their careers, according to the CCL, they have likely received help from multiple advisors in their personal and professional lives to hone necessary skills and gain confidence. Whether such advisors are mentors or sponsors, their assistance illustrates the important distinctions between the two types of roles:

- Sponsors tend to use their clout to help the individual secure assignments or projects that lift his or her visibility and responsibility within an organization. Mentors represent fertile ground for the individual to cultivate knowledge and advisement via their guidance on career-related decisions, opportunities, and challenges.
- The sponsor is an individual in the position to be able to successfully and favorably advocate for the "sponsee," given the sponsor's access to professional spaces that are typically closed to more junior and less seasoned employees or leaders. In contrast, the mentor relationship demands intentionality and buy-in from both participants: mentors must set aside the time to be responsive to the mentee's evolving and unique needs, and mentees must respect the mentor's time and take the initiative to maintain smart conversations and efficient dialogue.
- Largely, sponsors are senior leaders within their respective workplaces. Mentors have experience but can reside at various levels on the career ladder.
- Key actions undertaken and spearheaded by a sponsor revolve around advocacy and providing a tailwind behind a sponsee's career advancement to help her achieve potential. A mentor's primary actions or aims are to aid in the mentee's development and clarity of direction.

As articulated by the CCL'S Leading Effectively authors, the sponsor goes "above and beyond giving advice." In addition to touting the sponsee's accomplishments and potential, sponsors provide an abundant supply of encouragement to further instill self-confidence. Armed with confidence, those who are being sponsored are well positioned to take on challenging projects.

SPONSORSHIP: IMPORTANT FOR MALE LEADERS, CRITICAL FOR WOMEN

In a 2012 Catalyst report, researchers and authors Christine Silva, Nancy M. Carter, and Anna Beninger note that "crucial 'hot jobs' that advance high potentials further and faster" often involve large projects, high visibility, mission-critical roles, and international work. The report characterizes this reality as the "70/20/10 model":

- **70 percent** of development happens on the job
- **20 percent** of development happens through critical relationships
- **10 percent** of development happens through formal training programs

(Silva, writing with Herminia Ibarra in the *Harvard Business Review*, confirms this model, in that "big roles—more than formal programs—were the game changers when it comes to career advancement.")

Furthermore, the study suggests a key notion that formal leadership development programs can lead to the "hot jobs" that accelerate careers, *provided that those jobs are "managed strategically."* Conversely, formal programs do not always have the same connections to advancement, especially when the involved party is female.

In another nod to the nature of sponsor-endorsed "hot jobs," the female high-potentials whom Silva and Ibarra have been following landed fewer "game-changing experiences that ultimately predicted advancement than men did." Compared to their female counterparts whose careers have effectively stalled, the high-potential men bequeathed with game-changing opportunities boasted the following results:

- High-potential male leaders worked with budgets that were more than *twice the size* of the budgets that women were given in their respective projects or roles.
- The men in the study were also tasked with considerably more "people management"; their projects not only represented bigger-ticket investments but also were accompanied by *more than three times* as many staff members as the smaller-ticket projects of female peers.
- Approximately one-third of the men surveyed agreed with the statement that they had *received considerable C-suite visibility* while working on projects. Only one in four women in the study agreed with this statement.
- Men reported taking on projects with high levels of risk at greater rates than their female counterparts. This finding directly speaks to the lack of responsibility presented to women when male high-potentials are disproportionately placed in mission-critical positions of power and influence.

Discrepancies were quantified in at least five disciplines and types of roles: profit-and-loss (P&L) accountability, direct reports management, responsibility for budgets valued at more than $10 million, global team assignments associated with extensive travel (but not relocation), and international relocations. P&L, direct reports, and hefty budgets represent plum roles that are disproportionately held by men, sometimes by margins of up to 10 percent over women. The disparity is even greater for non-relocation global assignment opportunities and international relocation pursuits.

Within the confines of the formal programming space, women did exceed men in two key ways. They reportedly remained in leadership development programming longer, often starting in these developmental programs at younger ages and career stages than the men in their companies or organizations who were similarly deemed to demonstrate keen potential. Additionally, women were also more likely (at 47 percent) *to be assigned mentors in the first place* than men (at 39 percent).

As an example, Silva, Carter, and Beninger observed formal leadership development opportunities first being presented to women within 12 months of embarking on careers after their MBA programs. This is in marked contrast to the men who were not enrolled in similar programs until they were well into their early careerist phase—*two to four years* post-MBA. "More women . . . attended programs lasting one year or longer," the report notes, "while more men . . . were in programs lasting less than six months."

Interestingly, the tsunami of mentoring and advisement has failed to provide a positive ripple-effect in the area of *quality feedback*. The Silva/Ibarra study observes that despite the sheer volume of developmental exposure, women self-reported that the feedback they received was inferior to and less meaningful than the feedback qualitatively assessed by their male counterparts: "These programs can provide high-potential women and men alike with access to career-changing experiences that can get them ahead."

But the programs also represent "missed opportunities" when they have uneven outcomes, demonstrated by cross-functional, high-visibility, and stretch assignments clearly favoring one gender over the other.

DROWNING IN MENTORSHIP

"I am being mentored to death."

"Nathalie," a senior-level manager in the marketing department of a global consumer goods company, gave this grave statement to organizational behavior scholars Herminia Ibarra, Nancy M. Carter, and Christine Silva for their follow-up to an expansive Catalyst survey, titled "Why Men Still Get More Promotions than Women," featured in the *Harvard Business Review*.

Without firsthand knowledge via research or personal experience, it is easy to assume that Nathalie is prone to drama or hyperbole, especially if one falls within the demographic that has traditionally held the levers of power. However, with a deeper dive into Catalyst research spanning surveys of over 4,000 "high potentials," even those who are most distanced from inequities based on basic characteristics or identities can clearly see that Nathalie's distaste for conventional features of mentorship is more the rule than the exception.

The problem is not so much when mentoring is approached and evaluated with a broad brush. Rather, the sticking point resides with the *volume* and *quality* of the mentoring opportunities. Moreover, there may be a special something that is missing from these professional development experiences: sponsorship.

In turn, personal frustrations, played out in offices and workforces around the globe, and the lackluster results from structured development programs for women, are driven less by what is *present* within an organization and more by what is *absent* within respective businesses' structures and cultures. The problem is more about what is not being prioritized rather than what is at the front of often well-meaning leaders' minds when prioritizing initiatives theoretically designed to elevate women's representation as leaders within their workplaces.

Studies have shown that high-potential women earn significantly less than their male counterparts in their first post-graduate positions. Women are significantly less likely to be satisfied in their careers, in part because their male colleagues occupy higher-level management positions despite being comparably trained and experienced. Men are quite literally passing them by; they see it, up close and personal, and feel the sting.

In Nathalie's case, the merry-go-round of mentoring included a nudge from her boss to "raise her profile locally" while competing for a chairperson role within her home country. The boss asserted that the "excellent intracompany network" Nathalie established would be insufficient for her to land a more expansive, breakthrough role. She was encouraged to pursue active involvement with regional events and associations, too. This additional suggestion followed on the heels of Nathalie being matched with a high-level mentor, courtesy of a company program.

The *Harvard Business Review* article points out that Nathalie "had barely completed the lengthy prework assigned for that when she received an invitation to an exclusive executive-training program for high potentials—for which she was asked to fill out more self-assessments and career-planning documents. 'I'd been here for 12 years, and nothing happened,' observes Nathalie."

Nathalie and the other women surveyed by Catalyst were "not atypical." Companies were continuing to see leaky pipelines—talent seeping out of the organization and being lost at mid-level and senior-level stages of leadership.

When exploring the hurdles that persist and are even presented by organizational approaches to "support" and developmental programming, the heart of the matter is that not all mentoring is created equal. Interviews and surveys both indicate that high-potential women suffered from an onslaught of over-mentoring and under-sponsorship, especially as compared to male peers who are equally degreed and experienced yet disproportionately advantaged.

"[Women] are not advancing in their organizations," the trio conclude. "Without sponsorship, women not only are less likely than men to be appointed to top roles but may also be more reluctant to go for them."

One cannot help but reflect on all of the "Nathalies" of the world—*they are stuck*. They feel powerless. Disheartened. Exhausted. There are endless developmental commitments that compete for precious time, yet they rarely bear the fruit that is required for these ripe leaders' careers to blossom—at least not at the rate of their historically advantaged peers.

FAILURE TO FLOURISH

A stalemate is the point in a struggle or competition at which neither side is capable of winning and neither wishes to give in. No participant comes out ahead of another. The concept may seem curious to apply to the inequitable career situation faced by people of disadvantaged backgrounds or identities. After all, the clear winners in such a situation are the very individuals and power structures that have always remained at the top of the pyramid. However, as evidenced throughout this case for MSC, organizations stagnate when they do not evenly provide opportunities to equally high-achieving talent. That talent eventually rots on the vine.

Likewise, by failing to provide the mechanisms necessary for women and other traditionally disadvantaged groups to move forward in their careers, our society as a whole remains stagnant and does not progress. This regression is sustainable for only so long.

The disparities in access to career-defining and society-changing sponsorship engagement, activities, and roles underscore a truth: To combat the mechanisms that hold us back, we as leaders, organizations, and citizens must reflect on what got us here in the first place.

To begin with, sponsors and organizations must be aware of their blind spots. Women are challenged in their upward mobility by what Catalyst researchers describe as the "double-bind dilemma." Their summary puts it best: "Damned if You Do, Doomed if You Don't." The research in the report indicates that gender stereotypes plague women leadership with "several predicaments." "Because they are often evaluated against a 'masculine' standard of leadership," researchers write, "women are left with limited and unfavorable options, no matter how they behave and perform as leaders."

This research crystallizes these unfavorable dynamics into three predicaments, each of which presents a double-bind, undermines women's leadership, and limits options for career advancement. The first predicament involves extreme perceptions: women are rarely viewed as "just right" in their leadership roles. Instead, they are perceived as either overly soft or overly abrasive.

Second, female leaders are challenged by being held to a higher competency threshold than their male counterparts. Women do not reap rewards for adhering to a higher standard and demonstrating a sustained level of superior competency; rather, they continue to be rewarded in an inferior manner despite achieving and maintaining greater levels of proficiency in leadership.

Third, there is the lingering perception of a false dichotomy: to be famously competent or famously likable. To some people, the female leader who is both competent and well-liked is elusive. To someone of this mindset, women cannot have both qualities.

In addition to these three predicaments, the CCL has isolated notable reasons for the overabundance of men as sponsors *and* sponsees, and the dearth of women in both roles. These, too, must be identified and compensated for if progress is to be made.

- **The human tendency to like and gravitate toward others who are perceived as similar to us is a considerable barrier to diversity, equity, and inclusivity as a whole.** Men in leadership may, without realizing it, be inclined to champion and support other men. Because so much research confirms the value and impact of diversity, the wise leader is one who assesses his or her own network. Whom is the leader invested in developing? Whom has the leader endorsed, recommended, or been an ally for lately? Whose voices are they seeking out and nurturing to more accurately understand the climate and culture they exist in? What barriers can they identify that inhibit performance, engagement, and an inclusive environment?
- **A significant barrier to MSC opportunities in general, *unconscious bias*, has a profound effect on the golden sponsorship opportunities that pluck "stars" from relative obscurity within organizations.** Notably, leadership characteristics have for too long been naturally associated with qualities perceived as "male." This results in men who may not be as qualified or well suited to lead being automatically considered as "leadership material." The better-equipped, authentic "leadership material" gets passed by, simply because the individual identifies as a "she" rather than as a "he."

- **Women also get short shrift when it comes to assumptions about their personal and professional goals or preferences.** Instead of checking with the female leader herself and exploring at greater length her wants and needs, people with their hands on the levers of power often do not even consider women with the right qualifications and personal readiness for vital promotions and projects. Rather, these authorities make assumptions: "Jane has kids. The travel would be too demanding" or "Kate wouldn't want this job, because she'd have to uproot her family." While not vocalized, these dangerous assumptions result in the best person for the job being passed up, even though men have some of the same considerations—after all, they have families, too—yet are not stifled by such presumptions.

- **Emerging leaders tend to be reluctant to seek counsel, especially sponsorship, from individuals who appear to be "unlike" them in the most basic ways.** Thus, even when not accounting for other factors, the power structure remains stacked against women, people of color, and others who do not look like leaders traditionally at the top of businesses, political arenas, and other circles. To these emerging leaders I say, be courageous in advocating for yourself! Courageously initiate conversations, raise your hand for opportunities, and seek out the company of those whom you can learn from, collaborate with, and benefit from knowing.

KEY TAKEAWAYS

- Sponsorship is an active relationship, oriented toward the advancement of an individual.
- Sponsors are individuals who have more power or influence than you and will use it for you. They advocate

for you, endorse you, recommend you, and champion you in rooms and places where you are not or cannot be.

- Sponsors almost always have an existing mentoring relationship with their sponsee. The sponsor has been investing in them developmentally, and now they're activating a "mentor plus" relationship.
- Sponsorship is important for male leaders but absolutely critical for female leaders.
- Unconscious biases can influence mentoring and sponsoring relationships. Successful leaders intentionally pursue self-awareness and seek out feedback to discover where they might be in their own or others' way as they act as mentors, sponsors, or coaches.
- Myriad programs exist to develop leaders within organizations, but women are often over-mentored and under-sponsored. For this reason, these women are often not advanced into roles of increasing responsibility, visibility, and stature.
- Senior executive leaders should assess the individuals that they are investing in, with both mentoring and sponsoring, to ensure they're engaging with a diverse cross-section of the high potentials within their organization.

REFERENCES

Catalyst. 2007. *The Double-Bind Dilemma for Women in Leadership: Damned if You Do, Doomed if You Don't.* New York: Catalyst. See http://catalyst.org/research/the-double-bind-dilemma-for -women-in-leadership-damned-if-you-do-doomed-if-you-dont.

Ibarra, H., N. Carter, and C. Silva. 2010. "Why Men Still Get More Promotions Than Women." *Harvard Business Review.* Published September. http://hbr.org/2010/09/why-men-still-get-more -promotions-than-women.

King, M. D. 2021. "How Finding a Mentor—or Even Better, a Sponsor—Can Accelerate Your Career." *Yale Insights*. Published May 11. http://insights.som.yale.edu/insights/how-finding -mentor-or-even-better-sponsor-can-accelerate-your-career.

Leading Effectively staff. 2022. "Women Need a Network of Champions." Center for Creative Leadership. Published March 30. http://ccl.org/articles/leading-effectively-articles/why-women -need-a-network-of-champions.

Miller, J. 2020. "The People Who Can Open More Career Doors than You Ever Thought Possible." *The Muse*. Published June 19. http://themuse.com/advice/the-people-who-can-open-more -career-doors-than-you-ever-thought-possible.

Silva, C., N. M. Carter, and A. Beninger. 2012. *Good Intentions, Imperfect Execution? Women Get Fewer of the "Hot Jobs" Needed to Advance*. New York: Catalyst. See https://www.catalyst.org /research/good-intentions-imperfect-execution-women-get -fewer-of-the-hot-jobs-needed-to-advance.

Silva, C., and H. Ibarra. 2012. "Study: Women Get Fewer Game-Changing Leadership Roles." *Harvard Business Review*. Published November 14. http://hbr.org/2012/11/study-women-get -fewer-game-changing.

CHAPTER 7

What Works and What Doesn't in Sponsorship

TO ENSURE MAXIMUM impact, it is an absolute must for organizations to clarify their goals for development programs, aligning outcomes with objectives to guarantee that participating talent is developed in an equitable manner, using equal methods and means. Additionally, a distinction must be made between developing high potentials simply for the sake of "ticking a box" and pursuing an intentional strategy situated at the intersection of altruism and authenticity.

Consider, for instance, the following questions: Is your goal *just* to develop skills? Or is your team, department, or institution actually in need of more *equitable advancement*? Other considerations must be explored with the honesty, time, and brain space that they truly deserve.

If, for instance, the goal is to improve and accelerate advancement, how does one get the entire team on the same page that each high-potential individual is ready to embark on the next level? By achieving organizational clarity, answers to these questions can be used as a road map toward more effective, equitable delivery of development initiatives.

EXEMPLARS OF WORKPLACE EQUITY

In Catalyst's handbook, *Sponsoring Women to Success*, Heather Foust-Cummings, Sarah Dinolfo, and Jennifer Kohler isolate organizational case studies to further identify what has worked with this combination of well-considered, well-mapped mentoring plus "mentoring on steroids": sponsorship.

For instance, they spotlight Deutsche Bank's clarity of sponsorship expectations through its formal Accomplished Top Leaders Advancement Strategy (ATLAS) program. ATLAS reportedly prepares women for senior levels, both to improve balance at the top and to increase the number of women eligible for senior positions firmwide. These women are paired with members of the bank's Group Executive Committee (GEC). The GEC is sourced from a different business line, and each member is expected to "sponsor ATLAS women by championing them to lead the firm and advocating for them to fill senior most positions."

Reinforcing the strong business case for sponsorship, the authors note that Deutsche Bank leadership had realized that "companies employing more women in leadership positions are better able to attract and retain women employees and serve a diverse customer base."

In a nod to the impact of enthusiastic, top-down buy-in, the bank's then-CEO, Josef Ackermann, was the "ultimate sponsor" of the ATLAS program. As part of the enlistment process, he personally sent a letter to each woman, inviting her to attend an opening event and dinner. Ackermann was in attendance, as well as the GEC, which aided in providing tremendous visibility to these high-performing female sponsees.

ATLAS further made a point of identifying and elevating women leaders of diverse ethnicities, as well as participants from various functions and business lines, to more senior and more visible positions via "strategic sponsorship." In all, Deutsche Bank has paved the way for 45 percent of its ATLAS graduates to ascend to new or expanded roles within the organization.

These Catalyst findings further illustrate that women with *more* mentors were not necessarily the women who reaped the career advancement benefits that traditionally accompany such relationships. Rather, it was the accrual of *senior* mentors who could also double as *sponsors* that made all the positive difference for these women.

As Herminia Ibarra, Nancy Carter, and Christine Silva observe in "Why Men Still Get More Promotions than Women," other large, multinational organizations have walked this path. One can draw from those promising and favorable outcomes for inspiration and confidence that similar strategies, initiatives, approaches, and cultural attributes are an investment that will pay off, both financially and from a diversity, equity, engagement, and well-being standpoint.

For instance, the author-researchers refer to organizations such as Deutsche Bank, Unilever, Sodexo, and the European arm of IBM. These giants have also designed and deployed programs to "facilitate the promotion of high-potential women."

SPONSORSHIP IN ORGANIZATIONAL OPERATIONS

The literature is abundantly clear: sponsorship is an essential ingredient in career advancement for individuals and in the advancement of diversity, equity, inclusion, and overall organizational belonging.

How, then, should leaders undertake the task of embedding sponsorship more sustainably within their cultures?

Marissa D. King, the Yale University scholar and author, emphasizes how sponsors (unlike mentors) are "difficult (if not impossible) to assign." King continues, "Given the nature of the relationship, sponsorship has to be earned. When asked what it took to build relationships with three great sponsors, Sian McIntyre, the managing director of advocacy and customer experience at Barclays, put it succinctly: 'I've delivered.'"

King recommends taking stretch assignments that give one the opportunity to showcase one's skills:

> Other options are volunteering to take on roles and tasks that give you exposure to people you might not otherwise come across—organizing panels, writing special reports, or participating in programs to onboard new employees. However, performance and loyalty may not be enough to earn sponsorship. . . . You need to be able to differentiate yourself from peers.

Jo Miller of *The Muse* also emphasizes that getting to choose a sponsor is not how the process typically works. The sponsor almost always chooses you. Miller highlights six different ways to get the attention of influential sponsors:

1. **Channel the mantra of a shoe company giant and "just do it."** First comes great performance (the "doing"). Then comes the confidence that a sponsor can have in you and your exceptional work to put their own reputation on the line and advocate on your behalf.
2. **Do your due diligence.** Identify the good sponsors whom you want to attract. What makes for a great sponsor? Listen for talent developers who praise subordinates. Watch for talent scouts who back up others on contentious issues. Take note of those who are not stingy with offering assignments to up-and-comers.

3. **Raise your hand.** A surefire way to get noticed is to put yourself out there. Volunteer for special projects. Link up with the task forces or committees that those admired sponsors sit on. This step provides an opportunity for sponsors to see you in action.
4. **Don't be a "best-kept secret."** When seeking life-changing sponsors, this is not the time to hide your value. Make it visible. This could mean something as simple as mentioning an accomplishment that you are proud of when you catch up with would-be sponsors around the watercooler or in the cafeteria line.
5. **Establish clarity.** If you are wishy-washy about what you want for yourself, how can a sponsor support you? Plus, having clear goals for your career always makes the "asks" so much easier. You can consistently bring something specific to the table to drive difference-making conversations.
6. **Let your leaders in on your goals.** When your managers, mentors, and other leaders are aware of your performance and objectives, the enlistment of a sponsor occurs much more organically and smoothly. In fact, it can be a natural transition when managers or other leaders who are the sponsor's peers also talk you up and throw attention your way.

Elizabeth McDaid, senior vice president of leadership and management resources with The Council of Insurance Agents and Brokers, explored the other side of the aisle: best practices for the sponsor. In the aptly titled "How to Be an Effective Sponsor," appearing in The Council's *Leader's Edge* publication, McDaid writes that sponsors, too, must be on the lookout for high-potential talent. She further encourages others to seek out "overlooked leaders," looking for hidden talent. Many sponsors, she states, may use human resources departments as the vehicle to help them identify tomorrow's stars.

Additional savvy sponsor practices, as noted by McDaid, include the following:

- **Identify the best "stretch role."** Match profit-and-loss management roles, for instance, to the aforementioned "stars." Consider projects and roles that present some risk and allow sponsees to demonstrate their problem-solving abilities.
- **Tee up the role.** To combat "impostor syndrome," a protégé must know that they are valued, and they should be excited and willing to take on the assignment.
- **Nurture development and support.** A protégé will flourish when the right resources are in place to succeed. Consider and incorporate sufficient and appropriate expertise, time, and monies.
- **Lead the way.** Don't be stingy with your network. The very heart of sponsorship is in the connections and your willingness to introduce protégés to other influencers.
- **Provide quality feedback.** Performance assessments must be direct, specific, candid, results-driven, and conducted in consultation with the protégé's manager or supervisor.
- **Bolster resiliency.** Occasionally, a challenging project can result in a suboptimal outcome or take the wind out of an excited next-generation talent's sails. Don't let this seeming setback derail the sponsee. Success is not a single sprint from "A" to "B." It is a culmination of consistent, exceptional work, a journey characterized by many assignments and accomplishments. Lend this valuable perspective.
- **Promote and recognize high achievers accordingly.** This practice speaks to yet another defining element of the sponsor role: ensuring that others are aware of a deserving protégé's performance. Such visibility can lead to raises, promotions, and other forms of career-defining recognition.

INGREDIENTS FOR SPONSORSHIP SUCCESS

As much as the organization must weave together a supportive web of intentional initiatives, executives, and allies, the onus also falls on the individuals within each participating sponsor–sponsee relationship.

The report *Sponsoring Women to Success* highlights "Critical Features of the Sponsorship Relationship." In interviews of nearly 100 executives and high performers at six top multinationals, interviewees jumped wholeheartedly onto the **trust** bandwagon. Those respondents went so far as to call trust "the defining element" of good sponsor relationships. They indicated that this quality had to be present bidirectionally as a means of making the partnership successful.

Honesty was also seized upon as a critical feature. Leaders claimed that without it the sponsee could not receive the frank feedback so necessary to progressing within the ranks. As one sponsor put it, "I think an honest conversation [is critical]. So someone who's just not going to tell you what want you want to hear; someone [who] will tell you . . . the good, the bad, and the ugly."

Communication was described as the "vehicle for trust and candor." Protégés and sponsors alike emphasized the importance of freedom, openness, and confidence to speak honestly, straightforwardly, and completely.

Commitment is also a key differentiator between successful relationships and relationships that rot on the vine. Both parties must be dedicated to making the relationship work. A male protégé who was interviewed said that people who are "effective [at sponsoring] . . . their success is really your success. . . . They're really committed at a level of finding talent, and growing and developing that talent, and they're willing to make things happen for that talent."

CHECK YOUR BLIND SPOTS

I've mentioned during keynotes how, far too often, there may be a tendency for a mentor, sponsor, or coach to provide well-intended feedback or assistance. The problem is that while the intentions are good, the delivery may fail and results may fall short as the feedback is ineffectively communicated to a specific protégé or person. The circumstances or conditions that helped one person advance may not be realistic for another. The wise mentor/sponsor/coach is aware of these factors and intentional about considering them in their relationships and conversations.

Many pieces of advice from amazingly generous, seasoned male executives through the years undoubtedly worked well for them; however, these words of wisdom simply did not work for me and my situation as a female leader. This truth resonates even more for individuals from underrepresented groups. The concept of **intersectionality** acknowledges the unique lens that each of us looks through when experiencing all corners of the world, such as business, the law, healthcare access, and the ability to have a voice in public policy.

While reaching out to others who are unlike us in age, gender, race, ethnicity, or professional discipline breeds risk by its very nature, this diversity is critical in support and advocacy relationships. For many sponsors, there is the risk that their privilege will show in their counsel or recommendations. There is the risk that blind spots might result in a visible and uncomfortable gaffe or offense. What I tell leaders is that the wisest among us are in a constant process of challenging themselves to consider areas where they might "be in their own way" when doing good by the individual whom they are supporting. There remains an important element of sharing and learning that goes back and forth in these relationships, especially as the senior leader confronts potentially uncomfortable dynamics stemming from intersectionality and the varied viewpoints and life experiences that each individual brings to the workplace and the world.

As leaders in teams, departments, organizations, communities, states, and elsewhere, it is critical that we consider with clear eyes the potential realities of power and bias in day-to-day actions. Check your thinking. Adjust as needed. Don't be afraid to call out bias when you see it. The mere apprehension of calling out bias is indicative of bigger problems that must be addressed within the environments in which one works, lives, and plays. And to address those troubling problems, it is imperative that one first speaks up. Dialogue is just the start to dismantling the power structures and biases that hold us back, one organization or community at a time.

FOR THE SPONSEES

For readers who are seeking to be sponsored, it is critical to resist falling into the trap of thinking, "If I do a good job, people will notice. If I do more work or work harder, it will happen." Perhaps in a perfect world, all this goodness would happen and what is due to us would just come to us. The rewards would go to the high performers, the hard workers. But we all know the world is far from perfect.

Resist the tendency to get into your head too much or beat yourself up about leveraging sponsorship. It is not "cheating" or a "shortcut" to seek out some help—enlisting an ally to gain a promotion or position does not mean it was less earned. You don't deserve the role or responsibilities any less by having an enthusiastic senior decision-maker on your side who really wants to help you and derives pleasure from doing so.

Lastly, don't make the mistake of chalking everything up to timing, as in "It's not a good time for me right now. I'll go for the next opportunity." What makes for a "good time"? How does one know the "next opportunity" will come around? How long it will be before that next opportunity presents itself?

You are not alone. Countless others are thinking the same things right now and are wrestling with them—the source, no doubt, of many sleepless nights. There is beauty and power in access. Without networks of champions, progress can stall. Damaging behaviors, rooted in short-term frustration and a lack of perspective, can take hold and lead to long-term untoward consequences.

Mentoring, sponsoring, and coaching relationships, at the end of the day, are all about setting one up for the experiences that one needs to progress in one's career and to overcome the inevitable challenges along the way.

KEY TAKEAWAYS

- There is a compelling need for leaders to engage in mentoring and sponsoring in our organizations and professions.
- It is a must for organizations to assess their objectives for leadership development programs, ensuring equitable distribution and aligning resources to the intended outcomes.
- Unlike with mentoring, sponsorship connections are difficult to "assign." Rather, those mentor-plus relationships (see chapter 6) are earned.
- There are six ways to get the attention of influential sponsors:

  1. "Just do it."
  2. Do your due diligence.
  3. Raise your hand.
  4. Don't be a "best-kept secret."
  5. Establish clarity.
  6. Let your leaders in on your goals.

- Best practices for sponsors include the following:

  1. Identify the best "stretch role."
  2. Tee up the role.
  3. Nurture development and support.
  4. Lead the way.
  5. Provide quality feedback.

6. Bolster resiliency.
7. Promote and recognize high achievers accordingly.

- Trust, honesty, communication, and commitment are must-have attributes of successful sponsorship relationships.
- As a mentor, sponsor, or coach, beware the advice you give. Assess it for biases or blind spots that could cause your well-intended counsel to be ineffective, ill-fitted, or worse.
- As a high-potential, rising leader, be proactive and seek out relationships with those who can pour into you and aid your journey.

REFERENCES

Foust-Cummings, H., S. Dinolfo, and J. Kohler. 2011. *Sponsoring Women to Success*. New York: Catalyst. See http://catalyst.org /research/sponsoring-women-to-success.

Ibarra, H., N. Carter, and C. Silva. 2010. "Why Men Still Get More Promotions than Women." *Harvard Business Review*. Published September. http://hbr.org/2010/09/why-men-still-get-more -promotions-than-women.

King, E. B., W. Botsford, M. Hebl, S. Kazama, J. F. Dawson, and A. Perkins. 2010. "Benevolent Sexism at Work: Gender Differences in the Distribution of Challenging Developmental Experiences." *Journal of Management* 38(6). https://doi.org /10.1177/0149206310365902.

King, M. D. 2021. "How Finding a Mentor—or Even Better, a Sponsor—Can Accelerate Your Career." *Yale Insights*. Published May 11. http://insights.som.yale.edu/insights/how-finding -mentor-or-even-better-sponsor-can-accelerate-your-career.

McDaid, E. 2019. "How to Be an Effective Sponsor." Leader's Edge. Published September 16. http://leadersedge.com/brokerage -ops/how-to-be-an-effective-sponsor.

Miller, J. 2020. "The People Who Can Open More Career Doors than You Ever Thought Possible." *The Muse*. Published June 19. http://themuse.com/advice/the-people-who-can-open-more -career-doors-than-you-ever-thought-possible.

CHAPTER 8

The Value of Coaching

IN AN EPIC *New Yorker* piece, Dr. Atul Atmaram Gawande draws from his experiences as a top high school tennis player to thoroughly and memorably illustrate the importance of coaching to his career as a surgeon. Not all of us are surgical specialists, but most of us can relate to and learn from Gawande's motivations, processes, challenges, and personal and professional epiphanies associated when coaching moves from the court to the office, meeting room, or even the operating room.

After about six years as a surgeon, Gawande had reached the career stage where his performance in the operating room plateaued. He was prone to thinking, initially, of this realization as a "good thing." After all, Gawande had reached his professional peak. "But mainly," he writes, "it seems as if I've just stopped getting better."

Gawande compares this experience to his realization that his tennis game was steadily declining. The process that he instituted to address that issue would end up breathing new life into his performance in the operating room. During free time at a medical conference, he by happenstance ended up enlisting the aid of a 20-something college graduate and tennis coach. With just a few minutes of tinkering, Gawande said, the coach had added at least 10 miles an hour to his serve. "I was serving harder than I ever had in my life," he said.

This prompted Gawande to consider that nearly every elite professional tennis player, including Rafael Nadal, has a coach. All the pros use coaches to make sure they are as good as they can be. "But doctors don't," he observes. "I'd paid a kid just out of college to look at my serve. So why did I find it inconceivable to pay someone to come into my operating room and coach me on my surgical technique?"

Gawande then takes readers on a trip down memory lane to the dawn of coaching as a practice. It's a uniquely American development. The British were plagued by an ethos of amateurism associated with the aristocracy and hierarchical society. They deemed coaching and even practicing as "unsporting." But across the pond, a competitive and entrepreneurial spirit was taking hold. The legendary Walter Camp was enlisted as Yale's head coach for the then-fledgling American-rules football team. Position coaches were further established, and detailed performance records for each player were kept. Yale's rival Harvard, however, took the British approach to sport. And it showed—in every game they played in Yale's initial 30-year history, Yale beat Harvard all but four times.

Characterizing the coaching concept as "slippery," a nod to its potential nebulous or gray areas, Gawande provides one of the most well-articulated definitions of coaching as distinguished from other development partnerships that I have come across in my research:

> Coaches are not teachers, but they teach. They're not your boss—in professional tennis, golf, and skating, the athlete hires and fires the coach—but they can be bossy. They don't even have to be good at the sport. . . . Mainly, they observe, they judge, and they guide.

Gawande's observer, judge, and guide would come in the form of retired general surgeon Dr. Robert Osteen, under whom Gawande had trained during his residency. Osteen was one of the surgeons Gawande most wanted to emulate in his career. Osteen performed swift operations that didn't seem hurried. They were "elegant without seeming showy." Not once had Gawande seen his role model lose his temper. Osteen was remarkably well-planned for every situation, displaying "impeccable judgment." His patients had unusually few complications.

From the moment Osteen was invited to observe one of Gawande's surgeries for the first time—removal of a cancerous nodule (a procedure he had done "around a thousand times")—he offered eye-opening improvements for Gawande to incorporate. Even though this was a type of operation that Osteen had rarely done when he was practicing, he had plenty to tell Gawande. He admitted that they were small things but pointed out that worrying about the small things would help keep problems from occurring over time.

For example, Osteen noticed Gawande's inefficient positioning—how the draping may have been perfect for him but not for his surgical assistant across the table on the patient's right side. The assistant's left arm was restricted, which affected his ability to pull the wound upward. The draping further pushed the medical student off to the side so that he couldn't help at all. By making more room to the left (a small thing!), the student could hold the retractor, and the surgical assistant's hand would be freed up.

"He had a whole list of observations like this," Gawande said. "His notepad was dense with small print. . . . That one twenty-minute discussion gave me more to consider and work on than I'd had in the past five years."

Stranger still, Gawande said, *not a single senior colleague had observed him* in the eight years since he had established his surgical practice. "Like most work," Gawande notes, "medical practice is largely unseen by anyone who might raise one's sights. I'd had no outside ears and eyes."

COACHING AND PEAK PERFORMANCE

In many respects, Gawande is the ideal candidate for coaching. After all, as noted in our earlier introductory definitions to the concepts of mentorship, sponsoring, and coaching, the coach–coachee relationship is about refining and bettering the performance that has already been established and demonstrated.

By contrast, mentors and sponsors help establish you and get you to that peak performance. The mentor helps equip professionals with technical competencies, knowledge, and skills, while the sponsor helps others notice those technical competencies, engages the sponsored leader in new types or levels of work, and further unlocks the leader's potential.

The coach has the great joy of partnering with successful individuals who have reached plateaus or have their finger on the pulse of something very specific, such as weaknesses, sticking points, or obstacles that are holding them back from taking their peak performance to Everest-level heights.

For instance, leaders may look inward to consider how they can help their team become more productive as their efficiency or performance lags. Alternately, the journey toward a coach may start at the trailhead: examining how one could become more empowered or trustworthy. The leader may intuit or have others confirm to them that they micromanage or get overly lost in the weeds.

These specific challenges or identified weaknesses can lead to coaching. In fact, some of these scenarios point back to the helpful distinction between working *on* one's business or team while not working *in* the business or team. There is power in perspective, courtesy of partnering; in leveraging that perspective, there may be a capacity, passion, or level of performance that is unlocked within the coachee. One otherwise may not have known such talents or new heights existed. Such competencies and levels of performance simply may not have been previously accessible to the coached individual without the perspective and expertise of the coach.

I like to tell individuals that often the key differentiator between mentoring and coaching—and the defining component of coaching—is not the passing of wisdom, experience, and expertise. Rather, it can be classified as a process; the coach comes alongside the coachee and guides them to self-discovery.

The role of questions in a coaching relationship differs from their role in other mentoring relationships. In a mentor–mentee partnership, the mentor asks and answers questions to provide information and clarification. In contrast, coaches pose queries and hypothetical scenarios that inspire light-bulb moments, and the coachee answers or is encouraged to ponder the questions. This dynamic promotes real growth and transformation through introspection.

Coaching is, in turn, valuable because of a combination of characteristics and components, some of which are shared with the other types of relationships and developmental roles mentioned here. However, coaches go above and beyond "expertise." They serve as accountability partners and have smart feedback down to a science. In addition to opening up doors of introspection and self-discovery, coaches support growth by opening up new windows—a fresh perspective, just the antidote to narrow, small-minded subjectivity or self-limiting beliefs. These features then open up the leader to new opportunities and a level of technical aptitude and performance that otherwise would have been impossible or without the aid of a coach and all that relationship brings.

With that being said, there is real power in coaching that is combined with mentoring, just as there is an amplification effect with the combination of mentorship and sponsorship. As noted, former mentoring relationships often smooth the path to the skills that are necessary to be at a place where the goal is not to *build skills* but to *improve upon them* for new levels of success and impact. The mentor/coach approach presents a particularly robust net of vital threads in the form of wisdom, encouragement, validation, and camaraderie.

Coaching, still most synonymous with athletic prowess, is performance-driven to achieve a positive impact. Just as the Friday afternoon golfer or fitness junkie takes lessons or hires a coach to compete—or to improve their own personal performance regardless of the performance of others—the C-suite leader may find an executive coach to provide a valuable sounding board. Likewise, other professionals—whether they are transitioning to "being their own boss" or making a transition to another discipline or career—may enlist the appropriate business or career coach to best position them for success in a new niche or industry, and to make said transition as seamless and as smooth of a process as possible.

The desirable outcomes of coaching also include renewed engagement and innovation; enhanced performance in the leadership, business, and workplace realms; and the accountability to sustain desirable improvements in the coachee.

Successful, productive coaching relationships provide the following benefits:

- **Vision**—provides clarity of career objectives
- **Engagement and meaning**—provides clarity of purpose
- **Self-awareness and an understanding of strengths and weaknesses**—informs performance
- **Exhortation of a coach to help us do "hard things"**—promotes courage, accountability, and risk tolerance

On the path to progressing and performing, coaches also help the mental or physical "athlete" bounce back from perceived failures and adversity and even *learn* from those setbacks.

MANAGERS TURNED COACHES

While specific outcomes from coaching and specific characteristics associated with coaches may be identified, the relationship is not structured in any "universal" way; there are nuances, especially as we break through the traditional, more rigid mindsets associated with professional development methods and development-driven relationships.

There is a case to be made for empowering managers, even seasoned or previously coached leaders, to be coaches themselves. Management professor Monique Valcour, PhD, has gone so far as to say, "You can't be a great manager if you're not a good coach." This statement is the title of an article she wrote for the *Harvard Business Review* advancing the idea that "the most powerfully motivating condition people experience at work is making progress at something that is personally meaningful."

Valcour writes, "If your job involves leading others, the implications are clear: the most important thing you can do each day is to help your team members experience progress at meaningful work."

> "The single most important managerial competency that separates highly effective managers from average ones, is coaching."
>
> —Monique Valcour, PhD

Curiously, most companies have failed to integrate the critically important competency of coaching into managerial development and formal expectations of manager responsibilities. This disconnect has arisen despite the research showing that employees and job applicants alike embrace learning and career development above most other aspects of jobs.

After pointing out barriers to MSC relationships, Valcour surmises that managers are hand-wringing over a lack of time to take on the conversations and dialogue that represent valuable coaching. She theorizes that these managers may need the coaching and skill-building to facilitate such support and communication.

New York Times best-selling author Keith Ferrazzi also elevated the importance of coaching in managers in his article "Six Ways to Turn Managers into Coaches Again." Ferrazzi refers to transformations occurring within the world of workplace leadership that further reflect broader economic and societal change, writing:

> Historically, managers embraced the role of coach and mentor. . . . But today, tighter budgets, flatter organizations, a heavy workload, and too many direct reports often leave managers without the time—and sometimes without the skills—to shoulder the responsibility of being coach and

mentor. And yet, this function remains critical to the long-term health and productivity of the organization.

Ferrazzi highlights conversations—both formal and informal—between mentees and managers as being of particular value. Knowledge gained over spontaneous coffee breaks and one-on-one meetings can be worth more than information from textbooks or workshops.

Today, the dual and triple roles of manager/mentor and manager/mentor/coach have been eroded. It is a phenomenon that Ferrazzi (and many other thought leaders) have noticed:

> As part of a recent research project into how top executives view training and development programs, executives overwhelmingly said the most urgent problem they face is igniting their managers to coach employees. What's more, it's also the challenge where executives said they are most desperate to find and deploy effective solutions.

In the expansive article "The Leader as Coach" published by the *Harvard Business Review*, authors Herminia Ibarra and Anne Scoular state that companies are realizing managers cannot be expected to have all of the answers in the face of rapid and disruptive change.

"Once upon a time, most people began successful careers by developing expertise in a technical, functional, or professional domain," they write. "Doing your job well meant having the right answers. If you could prove yourself that way, you'd rise up the ladder and eventually move into people management—at which point you had to ensure that your subordinates had those same answers."

In the current work environment, it's still necessary that leaders have a solid foundation of competence in their given discipline in order to advance. However, the most effective organizations are intentionally seeking out individuals to promote into leadership roles who are more than simply the most proficient nurse, analyst, or project manager. Rather, organizations are looking for a foundation of credibility that's enhanced by a high level of proficiency in leading diverse teams, nurturing collaboration, and influencing outcomes through others. This style of leadership is less "command and control" and more "leader as coach."

This is a dramatic movement that Ibarra and Scoular have observed firsthand:

> When we talk about coaching, we mean something broader than just the efforts of consultants who are hired to help executives build their personal and professional skills. That work is important and sometimes vital, but it's temporary and executed by outsiders. The coaching we're talking about—the kind that creates a true learning organization—is ongoing and executed by those inside the organization. It's work that all managers should engage in with all their people all the time, in ways that help define the organization's culture and advance its mission. An effective manager-as-coach asks questions instead of providing answers, supports employees instead of judging them, and facilitates their development instead of dictating what has to be done.

Ibarra's and Scoular further cite the research work of emotional intelligence scholar, psychologist, and science journalist Daniel Goleman. In one of Goleman's classic studies of leadership styles from 2000, the leader-subjects classed coaching as their least favorite style. Their problem with coaching? They "simply didn't have time for the slow and tedious work of teaching people and helping them grow." This is increasingly common in healthcare and is exacerbated by nonstop meeting commitments and overwhelming numbers of direct reports.

In a study of 3,800 executives, 24 percent of those who were asked to "self-assess" their coaching skills "significantly overestimated their abilities." Compared to what individuals who worked for them said of their coaching prowess, the executives rated themselves as "above average" while their colleagues rated them "in the bottom third of the group." It's a telling mismatch and illustrates rather dramatically a lack of alignment between executives and their colleagues. Ibarra and Scoular emphasize that when the right tools and support are in place, almost anyone can be a better coach. Lots of practice and a sound method also play a vital role in improving the manager-turned-coach.

In fact, Ibarra and Scoular speak at length to these sound methods of coaching that can be employed. One such method is **directive coaching**, which is primarily facilitated through "telling" (what one typically thinks of as mentoring):

> Because it consists of stating what to do and how to do it, it unleashes little energy in the person being coached; indeed, it may even depress her energy level and motivation. It also assumes that the boss knows things that the recipient of the coaching does not—not always a safe assumption in a complex and constantly changing work environment.

This approach leans into rather rote, "traditional" teaching methods, whereby the teacher trains or directs the student. Such didactic teaching techniques do not harness adult learning theory built on experiential *doing and discovery* or on *discussions* between teacher and student. Neither do they embrace the acquisition of new skills through conversations and self-enlightenment, focusing instead on merely absorbing information imparted to them from the coach.

Additionally, the duo note that because leaders are allowed to "continue doing what they have always excelled at (solving other people's problems), it does not build organizational capacity well." This approach is often more time-efficient in the short-term, but it rarely equips the coachee to be self-sufficient in the long-term.

The authors describe the second method, **nondirective coaching**, as being built on listening, questioning, and withholding judgment. The coaches within this arrangement are equipped to draw wisdom, insights, and creativity from those whom they are coaching. Nondirective coaching empowers others to make all-important journeys of self-discovery, the very essence of what coaching is all about. The goal is to help those being coached to resolve problems and cope with challenging situations independently. In the nondirective mode, coaches can be "highly energizing," which is helpful for those being coached. But such coaching does not come naturally to most managers. There is the tendency instead to be most comfortable in the directive mode rather than the nondirective mode.

Lastly, Ibarra and Scoular identify **situational coaching**. Deemed by them as the "sweet spot," situational coaching has the manager-turned-coach straddle a fine balance between the directive and nondirective styles. This hybrid approach is dependent on the specific needs of the individual or direct report that is being coached and hearkens back to the ways that mentorship arrangements may be designed. One may recall "mentors of the moment," those individuals who fulfill specific needs with the passage of time and at various life stages. The coach, too, mayfulfill a specific need for the coached in the moment.

"From our work with experienced executives, we've concluded that managers should first practice nondirective coaching a lot on its own, until it becomes almost second nature," Ibarra and Scoular assert, "and only then start to balance that newly strengthened ability with periods of helpful directive coaching."

Ibarra and Scoular's recommendations for coaches nicely supplement Ferrazzi's own suggestions of practical tips for managers seeking to slip back into a coaching role. Ferrazzi's "Six Ways to Turn Managers into Coaches Again," lives up to its title by providing six practical tips as a means of helping managers to slip back into the role of coach, effortlessly and efficiently. These tips can be integrated by both managers and leaders. Broadly, they represent "best practices" that can characterize successful coaching relationships in general.

These practices, in no particular order, are as follows:

- **Check in, one-on-one, on a regular basis.** Waiting for annual performance reviews is not indicative of good coaching or support.

- **Let peer-to-peer coaching flourish!** You may recall the discussion of peer mentoring in chapter 5. The same concept can apply in the coaching realm. Generate more opportunities for other staff to further refine and elevate their talents, learning from each other in a meaningful and engaging group format. This is adult-learning theory in action! Ferrazzi: "It's also an easy way for you to coach multiple people at a time in one setting, thus maximizing your time and efficiency."

- **Channel the concept of "reverse mentoring."** The manager/coach can energize junior team members/coachees by providing opportunities for them to offer high-value insights into next-generation technologies and ways of thinking. The manager is also energized by learning new things, breathing new life into their respective roles and careers.

- **Tap the potential coach within others!** Ferrazzi suggests that coaching be encouraged across teams and departments by allowing individual members to host "mini-seminars" on topics that are important or that reflect the coach-in-training's passions or skill set. Get innovative; consider having these newbies create and share learning content and tips in private company spaces online.

- **Acknowledge and act on the importance of supporting day-to-day learning and development activities.** Ferrazzi enlisted the input of many Chief Learning Officers, who claimed that employees don't engage in learning opportunities "because they don't believe their managers would support them." To fight this perception and further support a healthy MSC culture, encourage employees to use office time to engage in learning. For instance, suggest that content be digested in small, manageable "bites" that can fit comfortably and seamlessly into staff schedules and workdays. Create enthusiasm around engaging ways to bring learning and development into the day-to-day.

- **Mind the formalities (in training).** As always, "hybrid" approaches and balance go far in driving positive transformations within individuals, organizations, and systems. Enhancements and improvements in hard and soft skills can be harnessed with the likes of formal training classes, certification programs, and executive education. The opportunities to learn and grow, given today's platforms and technologies, are seemingly limitless.

Valcour, too, understands why the current business environment has such a strong appetite for coaching. As she notes in "You Can't Be a Great Manager if You're Not a Good Coach":

> Can you teach old-school, results-focused line managers to coach their employees? Absolutely. And the training boosts performance in both directions. It's a powerful experience to create a resonant connection with another person and help her achieve something she cares about and become the kind of person she wants to be. If there's anything an effective, resonant coaching conversation produces, it's positive energy.

This notion of reciprocal exchanges in mentoring and coaching relationships plays out within the healthcare profession. Here, we can borrow from that mantra rooted in readying medical trainees, particularly those receiving surgical training: "**see one, do one, teach one**." After a trainee observes a surgical procedure, there is the expectation that they can then "do" or perform said surgery. Then, after the surgery has been performed or done, there is the expectation that the trainee will be able to "teach one"—that is, equip another trainee with the knowledge to perform that treatment.

In effect, there is a two-way street, with the trainee not only absorbing information from the coach but also passing that information on to the next trainee. There is much greater depth and complexity within the coach-coachee relationship, which transcends the common conception of a coach imparting knowledge to a junior-level leader but never encouraging that individual to show their growth through demonstration or education.

For Valcour's part, she has reportedly heard from "hundreds of executive students" that helping others learn and grow is among the most rewarding experiences they've enjoyed as managers. The effectiveness and joy that one has in the managerial experience can be significantly optimized by engaging in critical and surprisingly versatile coaching conversations with team members.

Valcour suggests harnessing the following complementary skill sets:

- **Listen.** There is power in deep validation that you, as manager or executive, demonstrate through complete focus on the coachee or staff member. Employ active listening. Open coaching conversations with queries such as, "How would you like to grow this month?" The exact verbiage is not as important as the intentional prioritization of attentive listening and the creation of connections that foster trust, openness, and creativity.
- **Ask, don't "tell" or "answer."** Consider the earlier terminology put forth by Ibarra and Scoular to define coaching methods and relationships; managers tend to be comfortable and more experienced with sharing in a *directive* style. Not to disparage the need for such styles and approaches, but there is a place for that style and other methods. The directive style better complements those clarifications when you are following up on projects or when individuals are actually seeking out your expertise. Coaching conversations are fertile ground for the *nondirective* manner. Be aware of any tendency to interject with answers or insights. These conversations are effective when, instead of having all the answers, the coach provides open-ended queries that provoke further introspection and considerations from the staff member being coached.

You play the role of guide rather than the all-knowing, omnipotent sage.

- **Create a coaching or developmental alliance and sustain it.** This step hearkens back to Ibarra and Scoular's notion of "situational coaching": development opportunities that evolve as the student evolves and that address specific needs or activities in the moment. The savvy healthcare leader-coach nurtures partnerships with colleagues across disciplines and team environments, harnessing the diversity and creativity resulting from a more collaborative approach. Much of the onus in coaching relationships ultimately falls back on the team member seeking improvement, hopefully within an environment set by their team/department/organizational leader. So a scenario that involves the employee directing the path forward illustrates the very heart of these relationships.

- **Steer toward the positive.** The purpose of this skill is not to ignore potentially weak areas but to ensure that the conversation doesn't become mired in complaints and negativity, especially when the coach and coachee can do nothing to resolve these complaints and sore spots. As Valcour puts it, "Venting can provide temporary relief, but it doesn't generate solutions." The best approach, she suggests, is to acknowledge the frustrations as a means of deep and active listening. Then, encourage the employee to move forward and past them. A great coaching question to ask in these circumstances is "What would have to be true?" Prompting your coachee to consider a solution-oriented direction can often lead to options that can be acted upon.

- **Mind the accountability.** As an accountability partner in addition to coach and manager, one should create a system or plan so that the employee is held to it to form and implement developmental strategies. A plan might include identifying next steps, anticipated milestones, as well as their accompanying time frames. Include any investments that must be made on the part of the institution to make those opportunities happen, and chart a plan for follow-up that confirms progress.

Largely, coaching aids in bolstering robust and meaningful bonds between managers and the broader team. These relationships furthermore encourage associates to consider the ownership that they are taking of their professional development and to build themselves up in this arena. As with some of the world's most talented coaches in the sports world, in the business world you, too, can help the "student" or "mental athlete" take their performance to its peak or pinnacle.

It certainly wouldn't be the first time that sports metaphors have been used to describe the coaching experience. Valcour recalls an executive at one of her global coaching workshops who described the process as akin to extreme sports, saying the coaching exercise felt "like a bungee jump."

"I was delighted to see that this man," she says, "who had arrived looking reserved and a bit tired, couldn't stop smiling for the rest of the evening. He was far from the only participant who was visibly energized by the coaching experience."

Coaching is a vehicle to effect cultural transformation. Healthcare leaders can articulate why coaching is so valuable, both for each professional and for the respective organization as a whole. Leaders must be tasked with embracing and modeling coaching, building coaching capacities through varied ranks and ladders of the organization, and removing any barriers to transformative change and the integration of coaching into the fabric of an institution's culture.

As Ibarra and Scoular state:

We live in a world of flux. Successful executives must increasingly supplement their industry and functional expertise with a general capacity for learning—and they must develop that capacity in the people they supervise. No longer can managers simply command and control. Nor will they succeed by rewarding team members mainly for executing flawlessly on things they already know how to do.

Leaders, play the long game. Commit to a coaching approach that delves into and unlocks the potential in others. It may take longer than a day, a week, a month, or even a year. But over time, your investment will yield a return. Those outcomes are where true impact can occur at scale.

KEY TAKEAWAYS

- Coaches provide outside eyes and ears, a valuable perspective that we lack.
- Coaching is performance oriented.
- Coaches have valuable expertise, but often they're not giving the coachee all the answers. Rather, coaches guide them to a place of self-discovery.
- Coaches are in a position to offer valuable feedback that allows the coachee to refine their approach, elevate their performance, and improve their outcomes.
- One of the most valuable parts of mentoring and coaching others is helping them gain clarity around their unique and individual purpose, strengths, vision, values, and goals.
- Many leaders feel ill-equipped to coach, overestimate their coaching abilities, or lack the bandwidth to invest in coaching their team members.
- Best practices for coaching in the workplace include the following:
  - Check in, one-on-one, on a regular basis.
  - Let peer-to-peer coaching flourish.
  - Engage in reverse mentoring/coaching.

- Tap the "potential coach" within others.
- Acknowledge the importance of supporting day-to-day learning and development.
- Invest in training.

REFERENCES

Ferrazzi, K. 2015. "Six Ways to Turn Managers into Coaches Again." *Harvard Business Review*. Published August 10. https://hbr.org /2015/08/6-ways-to-turn-managers-into-coaches-again.

Gawande, A. 2011. "Personal Best." *The New Yorker*. Published September 26. https://www.newyorker.com/magazine/2011 /10/03/personal-best.

Goleman, D. 2005. *Emotional Intelligence: Why It Can Matter More Than IQ*, 10th-anniversary ed. New York: Random House.

Ibarra, H., and A. Scoular. 2019. "The Leader as Coach." *Harvard Business Review*. Published November. https://hbr.org/2019 /11/the-leader-as-coach.

Valcour, M. 2014. "You Can't Be a Great Manager If You're Not a Good Coach." *Harvard Business Review*. Published July 17. https://hbr.org/2014/07/you-cant-be-a-great-manager-if-youre -not-a-good-coach.

CHAPTER 9

Coaching for Performance:
Sharpening the "Professional Game"

Dr. Ruth Gotian, in "How to Turn Feedback into an 'Opportunity for Enhancement'" for *Forbes*, encourages those who are receiving feedback within coaching or similar relationships to "think like an Olympian." She refers to the experience of Olympian fencer Iris Zimmermann, who says of her constant fine-tuning, "Athletes crave constant feedback because one small adjustment can be the difference between crossing the finish line first or second—or in the case of fencing, the difference between hitting the target and getting hit."

Gotian furthermore encourages both coaches and those being coached to rethink the way that they look at receiving and giving feedback. There are few words, she notes, that inspire more cringing than "Would you like some feedback?" Automatically, we start to get defensive. Our bodies shut down. Comments are not heard when one gets off to such a sour, anxiety-inducing start.

"The problem is that we are viewing it all wrong," she continues. "We automatically think people will tell us what is wrong with our idea or proposal. I suggest that we reimagine feedback as an 'opportunity for enhancement.'"

Gotian says that the language one uses within this process must be considered carefully. *Words matter.* One doesn't even have to use the word "feedback." Instead, opt for something casual like "I have some thoughts on how to expand your great idea." Doesn't that automatically sound so much better to the hearer? Instead of shuddering at the proposition that they will be criticized, the coachee is now excited and eager to hear about ways to get their ideas scaled and to increase their presence and reach.

Gotian also cites the recommendations of Deborah Grayson Riegel, a leadership communications consultant and educator. Riegel suggests focusing on "measurable, observable, and repeatable" behaviors, not personality or character:

> For example, if someone routinely interrupts people, consider suggesting that to have a lasting impact, they should let everyone else speak first, summarize what they heard, and then give their recommendation. Telling someone they are rude is of little value, telling them how to get their message heard is much more useful.

Feedback, no matter how one attempts to dress it up with less intimidating verbiage, ultimately comes down to a positive: The best of intentions are at work. The coach wants to *enhance* and not *criticize* one's work. When their charge does better, the coach does better, and the team, department, division, and entire organization follow suit.

Olympic fencer Zimmermann has mastered the art and science of implementing well-intentioned guidance into her sport: "The foundational element to receiving and adapting to feedback is an unshakable confidence in one's own capabilities and one's own ability to put the feedback into practice." Zimmermann's words illustrate a key distinction between coaching and other forms of mentorship:

Those who are being coached often have demonstrated exceptional capabilities and abilities. They are confident in their existing skills and talents. They just need to take external insights and internalize them as a means of improving. A top regional competitor can become a top national competitor, and a top national competitor can become an Olympic-caliber competitor.

Speaking of positives, Gotian encourages all of us to consider the last time feedback or a critique involved a positive statement. No wonder why feedback has such a black mark. It is associated with so much negativity. The very word makes individuals squirm. While discomfort can often inform growth, feedback should not be so all-or-nothing. It must have areas of gray and offer room to highlight the good in those whom we collaborate with and coach.

One way to deliver such praise is to sincerely convey how a charge's attention to detail and conscientiousness positively affects the coach and other members of the team. However, praise can also make the individual who is being coached squirm in their seats a bit. Often, this is because it is infrequently provided to them, which suggests a weakness in the traditional process of viewing and providing feedback. Gotian credits authors Marshall Goldsmith and Sally Helgesen (*How Women Rise*) with recommending that the response to praise be simple and straightforward. All one has to say is "Thank you." That's it. Stop. Do not say, "I couldn't do it without my team" or "It was nothing!" By responding to feedback that way, the "traditional" way, the coachee is either minimizing their role in the project or achievement or minimizing the very project or accomplishment that is being spotlighted. Accept positive feedback graciously.

A certified executive coach herself, Meg Myers Morgan, PhD, notes in her article "Five Essential Ingredients for a Successful Coaching Relationship" that one must resist the temptation to view this partnership as a "vending machine," in which one inserts money and a product comes out, neatly packaged.

"Coaching is *relational*," Morgan stresses. She offers "five essential ingredients" for a healthy coaching relationship.

To maximize the coaching experience and opportunity, Morgan first recommends **commitment**: the motivation, resolve, and investment that are required to take on a specific obstacle or situation. For example, the coaching experience should not be prompted by an empty motivation to "please my boss." Rather, the motivation should be to resolve conflict or support improved dynamics in the workplace.

Second, Morgan puts perhaps the most precious of resources, **time**, on a pedestal. She notes that, as I often teach, coaching and other professional-development experiences are frequently pushed into the margins. They may be the first commitments to be delayed or canceled, as already packed schedules become more so. As Morgan points out, "Time [for one's coach] must be allotted, protected, and honored for the process to work." After all, deep and meaningful coaching is built on a foundation of time. It does not occur overnight, just as experiences that are truly worth our time rarely fall into the "instant gratification" category.

Third, **coachability** gets to the very essence of the coachee's responsibilities and desirable traits within the coaching relationship. The person being coached must be genuinely open to it. This is not a "fake it till you make it" situation, as coaching requires earnest participation from the recipient, whose spongelike absorption of key information and guidance will lead to further success.

Chemistry, the fourth essential trait, hearkens back to our earlier discussions of how organic relationships are built in the leadership development sphere on a foundation of gelling as individuals. Chemistry is not driven by cognition. Rather, it is something that we *feel* as participants. All of us bring different histories, backgrounds, personality characteristics, and other factors to each relationship. So if one doesn't feel as if the coach is "clicking" with them, it's OK to seek out a coach who has a different communication style. As a coach myself, however, I recognize the importance of discussing concerns before "coach-hopping." We can then evaluate, together, whether the concern may be effectively addressed within our relationship. All that may be necessary is a simple course correction with the same coach to move forward and ascend.

Last but not least, we return to the vital element of **trust**. This is an all-important facet of relationships, including physician–patient, peer-to-peer, and coach–coachee. Progress cannot be achieved unless there is a level of trust in the coach's competency, training, honesty, and commitment.

FEEDBACK AS FUEL

"Rest at the end, not in the middle. I'm always chasing that win. Never done." Regularly lauded as one of the top professional basketball players of all time, the late Kobe Bryant has been credited with this statement. Bryant is very much the embodiment of what it takes to go from "average" or even "good" to "great" or "exceptional." Gotian, writing again for *Forbes* in her article "Why Kobe Bryant and Michael Jordan Kept Winning on and off the Court," consulted with legendary coach, personal trainer, and motivational speaker Tim Singh Grover to explore this phenomenon.

You see, Grover had the astounding privilege of training some of the top basketball players of all time, among them Bryant, Jordan, and Dwayne Wade. He relates his experiences with these legends in *Winning: The Unforgiving Race to Greatness*. Grover notes that these players' journeys to the uppermost echelons of athletic excellence were based on 13 distinctive "winning" principles or mindsets. There is no particular order to integrate these mindsets or principles into one's life and training; the idea is just to ensure that *all* principles are accomplished at some point or other. These items can just as easily be applied to the high-performing, never-stop-learning CEO's day-to-day as they are integrated into the unstoppable professional athlete's routine.

For instance, Grover encourages the relentless pursuit of pushing oneself harder even as everyone else has had enough. One can shrug off failure, knowing that there is more than one way to "get what you want," and avoid resting on one's laurels: "You don't celebrate your achievements because you always want more."

Grover also provides some eye-opening insights into his relationships with all of these greats. For example, he recalls how Bryant would often phone him at 3 a.m. The basketball star would ask what Grover was doing. "Sleeping" was, naturally, his answer. But before long, Grover realized that Bryant tended to call him in certain cycles or patterns. He would know when to expect the call and would be ready at the gym for those moments when Bryant needed him the most. They would then work together to fix whatever was missed in the last game. Grover says, "Bryant never focused on his success; instead, he fixated on what he missed." It is from this endless pursuit of improvement that 3 a.m. calls and 4 a.m. workouts at the gym flowed.

Many of the same characteristics were shared by Bryant's "mentor" of sorts: Michael Jordan. Instead of having a stat sheet that highlighted his positives (baskets, passes, rebounds), Jordan had a stat sheet that highlighted the negatives: the baskets that were missed, the fouls that were made, the balls that were turned over. Jordan focused on the "micro-changes," regardless of how successful he was in the moment.

In keeping with Gotian's experience, these elite players all craved feedback. Such athletes don't see such input as a negative critique. Their feelings are not hurt by it. They see it as fuel, an opportunity to enhance their skills and to outplay and outperform others who are nipping at their heels.

Arguably one of the most telling episodes in the Grover–Jordan relationship occurred at the very start of the relationship. Before the internet and e-mail, Grover would introduce himself to all of the Chicago Bulls players with earnest, handwritten letters that extolled his "winning formula," derived from extensive training and skills-building in the areas of kinesiology and exercise science. As Gotian writes:

> The only person [Grover] did not send a letter to was Michael Jordan because he did not think the best player in the NBA would want his services. Jordan saw the letter in a teammate's mailbox and was the only one who sought out Grover's additional training. He wanted something different and more than all the other players.

As Grover emphasizes, "winning" is not about achieving something *once*. It is, instead, the ability to achieve something *repeatedly*. His anecdotes may pertain to elite NBA players, but there are lessons to be gleaned that transcend the industry and can be applied to almost any space, role, or position. Many of those lessons center on the will to "win" through putting in the work and the time.

COACHING CULTURE: PERK OR PENALTY

Marshall Goldsmith, one of the authors referenced in chapter 5's exploration of coaching, is also a pioneer in the development of metrics to quantify the leadership development process, progress, and outcomes. His article "Coaching for Behavioral Change" pulls back the curtain on how he uses this tool and others while partnering as a coach with clients and their managers.

At the beginning of each relationship, Goldsmith solidifies an agreement with clients and other involved managerial parties to suss out answers to the following questions: *What are the key behaviors that are poised to most positively change and increase the effectiveness of leadership? And who are the key stakeholders responsible for assessing progress on those changes 12 to 18 months later?*

Their 360-degree feedback tool is designed to measure changes in behavior among executives who were provided with feedback. Within this framework, Goldsmith's team later follows up with those participating execs and their teams to see how such recommended insights have been integrated.

Goldsmith's team only gets paid after clients have achieved positive changes in key, identifiable behaviors. This itself was isolated as a positive differentiator and evolution in the coaching model. Goldsmith says that leadership coaches are often paid for the wrong reasons; their income is largely predicated on the questions "How much do my clients like me?" and "How much time is allocated toward coaching these clients?" Neither of these factors represent the metrics that inform positive and sustained behavioral change. There is no correlation, according to Goldsmith, between "being liked" and executives' changes in behavior (the results). In fact, he asserts that if coaches become too concerned about their likeability, "they may not provide honest feedback when it is needed."

As to the time element, the executives Goldsmith's team works with are all decision-makers responsible for billions of dollars. "Their time is more valuable than mine," he says. "I try to spend as little of their time as necessary to achieve the desired results."

In his work with some of the world's leading CEOs, Goldsmith isolates a few truisms that link all of those coaches. For one, they are universally motivated to improve. They are also not only asking everyone else to improve; they recognize there is always room for self-improvement and that they are not perfect. No one is.

Goldsmith also notes that his team works with leaders who potentially have great futures within said corporations, *not* with those who have been written off. These execs are not being fired. They are engaging in a "pseudo behavioral coaching process" designed less to "help people get better" and more to "seek and destroy" perceived problems.

This approach indicates a misperception about coaching and motivations for coaching that is fraught with landmines. This misperception arises from coaching culture being viewed as a punishment rather than a perk.

Efforts to instill coaching into an organization's culture can be looked upon as either a positive (development-oriented) or a negative, making the coached individuals feel as if they are "problems" who need to be fixed. They may feel as if they are being singled out for extra attention because they are underperforming.

This sentiment about coaching, understandably, generates an abundance of resistance, speculation, and negativity toward the process. Conversely, the healthy perceptions of (and motivations behind) coaching are instilled. Coaching is understood as an opportunity to elevate the performance and capacity of leaders deemed as "high-performing" who have so much more room to grow.

In turn, leaders ought to be mindful of how their respective organizations are approaching team members with the proposition of coaching, and of how they are "framing" these efforts within multifaceted communications strategies. Those who are responsible for integrating such efforts into the organization's cultural fabric must honestly evaluate and ask themselves why they are so interested in investing in these opportunities.

Additionally, Goldsmith makes the distinction between leadership-behavior coaching and other types of coaching, which range from strategic coaching to life planning. And he emphasizes that executives with integrity violations should be *fired* and not steered toward being *coached*. Again, this highlights how coaching (properly understood) is meant to provide support and further improve great performance rather than serving as a tool to punish or "fix" ineffective leaders.

At this phase of Goldsmith's coaching career, he spends more time with the *key stakeholders* surrounding an executive than he does with the coaching recipient. These stakeholders are enlisted to aid the coached executive. They should be encouraged to let go of the past that cannot be improved upon and instead focus on the future that is amenable to change. Think of it as "feedforward" instead of "feedback"! Key coworkers should be helpful and supportive and should resist the temptation to be cynical, sarcastic, or even judgmental about the process—negative behaviors that hold the exec and the whole team back.

Goldsmith wants these stakeholders to be candid with him. When they follow up 18 months or so later, he doesn't want them to paint an inaccurately rosy picture. He wants their genuine, unvarnished observations and opinions about the executive's growth and progress (or lack thereof). Occasionally, Goldsmith's team receives a glowing report that curiously doesn't match up with reality, only to hear the truth far later: "He didn't get better. We just said that." As Goldsmith notes, lying about progress is "not fair to my client, to the company or to me."

There is an endpoint to the entire process. The formalities cease when results have been achieved. Goldsmith emphasizes that the goal is not to create a "dependency relationship" between coaches and clients. Although he almost always keeps in touch with "graduates" in different ways for the duration of their lives, these interactions do not always occur within the confines of an ongoing formal coaching relationship.

In yet another nod to the cultural implications of behavioral change through coaching, Goldsmith concludes that increasing one's abilities to lead people can be even more impactful when viewed through the framework of a "20-year process" rather than a one-year program. And even the most seemingly stubborn of executives and leaders among us can change. After all, Goldsmith only gets paid when leadership changes. And his team almost always gets paid! Goldsmith's words recall the concept of micro-refinements in elite athletes' sports games:

> "At the top of major organizations even a small positive change in behavior can have a big impact. From an organizational perspective, the fact that the executive is trying to change leadership behavior (and is being a role model for personal development) may be even more important than what the executive is trying to change. One key message that I have given every CEO that I coach is *'To help others develop—start with yourself.'*" [Emphasis added.]
> —Marshall Goldsmith

COACHING: YOUR OUTSIDE EARS AND EYES

Bringing this all back around to Atul Gawande, the surgeon-author from chapter 8, Gawande discusses at length the evolution of his relationship with his coach and senior role model, Dr. Robert Osteen. Osteen saw that Gawande was noticing the small things more quickly, such as when direct illumination drifted out of wounds during procedures. Gawande caught this oversight in four minutes, rather than 30 minutes (his former record when confronted with a similar situation).

Gawande sums up, "Since I have taken on a coach, my complication rate has gone down. It's too soon to know for sure whether that's not random, but it seems real. I know that I'm learning again. I can't say that every surgeon needs a coach to do his or her best work, but I've discovered that I do." Gawande highlights a favorite saying of Osteen's: "Most surgery is done in your head."

Osteen was driving Gawande to make smarter decisions at a bit of a price: the uncomfortable risk of exposure and being vulnerable. Many of Gawande's colleagues who were approached with the concept of coaching enthusiastically declared that they knew of many *others* who could really use the coaching. But did they ever offer up themselves and their need for a coach? No.

Gawande continues:

> For society, too, there are uncomfortable difficulties: we may not be ready to accept—or pay for—a cadre of people who identify the flaws in the professionals upon whom we rely, and yet hold in confidence what they see. Coaching done well may be the most effective intervention designed for human performance. Yet the allegiance of coaches is to the people they work with; their success depends on it. And the existence of a coach requires an acknowledgment that even expert practitioners have significant room for improvement. Are we ready to confront this fact when we're in their care?

It can be intimidating to ask for coaching or trust our colleagues to do the same. As leaders, we want and need to be seen as competent, credible, and capable. But none of us is perfect. We all have more to learn and room to grow. Modeling the humble pursuit of improvement is the most effective way that we can inspire others to do the same.

KEY TAKEAWAYS

- Effective coaching relationships require five essential ingredients: commitment, time, coachability, chemistry, and trust.
- An attribute that separates high achievers from average achievers is a relentless thirst for feedback that informs growth.
- Coaching is a perk, not a penalty. It is an investment in the continued positive performance of high-potential leaders, not a punishment for "problem children" in your organization.

- To drive behavioral change, think of input as "feedforward" instead of "feedback."
- Leveling up in leadership requires our ability to be very candid with ourselves about our current reality. The most effective executives welcome honest feedback and surround themselves with those who will share the unvarnished truth, no matter how painful.

REFERENCES

Gawande, A. 2011. "Personal Best." *The New Yorker*. Published September 26. https://www.newyorker.com/magazine/2011/10/03/personal-best.

Goldsmith, M. 2017. "Coaching for Behavioral Change." MarshallGoldsmith.com. Accessed October 20, 2022. http://marshallgoldsmith.com/articles/coaching-for-behavioral-change-2.

Gotian, R. 2021. "Why Kobe Bryant and Michael Jordan Kept Winning on and off the Court.'" *Forbes*. Published May 18. http://forbes.com/sites/ruthgotian/2021/05/18/why-kobe-bryant-and-michael-jordan-kept-winning-on-and-off-the.court.

———. 2020. "How to Turn Feedback into an 'Opportunity for Enhancement.'" *Forbes*. Published August 14. https://www.forbes.com/sites/ruthgotian/2020/08/14/how-to-turn-feedback-into-an-opportunity-for-enhancement.

Morgan, M. 2021. "Five Essential Ingredients for a Successful Coaching Relationship." *Chief Learning Officer*. Published February 12. http://chieflearningofficer.com/2021/02/12/5-essential-ingredients-for-a-successful-coaching-relationship.

CHAPTER 10

The Practice of Self-Coaching

THE CONCEPT OF "self"—self-awareness and the ability to coach and motivate oneself—is critical. After all, to lead others well, we must first know and lead ourselves well (a nod to Dr. Daniel Goleman's Emotional Intelligence model). The practice of self-coaching consists of a hearty helping of reflection, the pursuit of feedback, leading by example, and a never-ending hunger to grow (reading, learning, listening to podcasts, enrolling in professional development programs, etc.). As with other relationships and efforts explored throughout this book, one must be intentional in embarking on these behaviors and in practicing them to reach new heights of self-understanding and leadership prowess. There is much to be said for baring one's own understanding of self to others—for being vulnerable and courageous in communicating to those around us our shortcomings and natural proclivities, right alongside our strengths and the discoveries that inspire the individuals we lead, mentor, sponsor, coach, organize, lift, and motivate around shared goals.

Executive coach Ed Batista has produced a large body of literature on behaviors related to equipping others with self-coaching skills. He even teaches the "Art of Self-Coaching" class at Stanford University. His description of self-coaching in his article "Self-Coaching Is Social" flies in the face of assumptions about undertaking coaching solitarily, which also raises the question as to how one can be coached without another party to function as the coach:

> "Self-coaching is a *self-directed* process, in that we're taking active responsibility for guiding our own growth and development, but other people play extremely important roles in this process at every step."
>
> —Ed Batista

Self-directed processes may include solitary activities such as journaling that encourage reflection on items both small ("What am I feeling right now?") and large ("What do I want to do with my life?"). It is essential for leaders and nonleaders alike to engage in these practices and provide breathing room within packed schedules to support them. As for the "social" dimensions of self-coaching, Batista notes that "solitary activities are just one aspect of a self-coaching process that also involves meaningful relationships with others." He encourages readers to consider how even the most beloved partners within our circles can sometimes offer up well-meaning but decidedly unhelpful counsel or advice. Think of the life partner who tries to cheer you up after a professional setback: Their response may be to say, "Look on the bright side . . ." or to fall back on their knowledge of situations that are wholly different than yours ("When I encountered . . ." or "I solved ____ by doing this . . .").

The solution to this tendency, Batista asserts, is to employ coaching tools and techniques that enable more effective "helping conversations." Of course, to support better assistance and conversations requires highly social and interactive pairings of students, as well as small group gatherings to replicate real-world conditions and more effectively dole out and receive coaching support.

STRENGTHS-BASED LEADERSHIP

In my workshops and classrooms, I am a big advocate for leadership that is driven by an understanding of each individual charge's unique strengths. I like to provide an active exercise for my clients. I tell them to jot their signature down on a piece of paper as many times as possible in ten seconds using their dominant hand. Then I have them write their signature as many times as possible with their nondominant hand on the other side of the paper.

Unless the client is among the 1 percent of the population that is truly ambidextrous, the two sides of the paper look dramatically different, with one legible side featuring more signatures and the other side resembling a four-year-old's scribbles. I don't offer this exercise simply for the client's health but rather to demonstrate the power that resides within each of us to identify and hone our natural strengths and talents. There are real implications for the bottom line and employee well-being when professionals struggle within jobs or cultures that primarily require the application of one's weaknesses. In this soul-sucking situation, each employee's strengths are not allowed to shine through or be refined.

Although we can openly acknowledge our weaknesses as a means of improving, we have greater opportunity for improvement by building on personal talents, which often go hand in hand with areas of interest and passion. When we are allowed to apply, shine, and grow with these strengths and interests, we achiever higher performance and are likely more engaged in our work and work-places. Additionally, others begin to rely on us and our unique set of abilities. The true and enthusiastic performance that is unlocked with strengths-based leadership and organizational cultures is contagious and inspiring to those who depend on us so much and look up to us.

As with all things, even features as seemingly positive as strengths, there is a dark and light side. This is where the concept of *managing strengths* comes into play. I, for one, am deeply relational. I love getting to know others better and contributing to their lives and organizations in a positive way. In the past, when personal and professional relationships have not been reciprocal, it has been a considerable source of disappointment (and subsequent learning) for me. It is important in these circumstances for me, and all of us when evaluating what makes us tick and grow stronger, to consider that old chestnut: we can have "too much of a good thing." Sometimes, our greatest strengths—the very elements that contribute to making us our best selves—can also have a tendency to occasionally place us at our worst.

When encountering situations or dynamics that call for tempering or managing those strengths, I recognize that, in putting myself out there for others and connecting deeply and meaningfully, there will always be risks. My perspective and preference may be unvalued or unrealistic for another. But these are risks I am more than willing to take. We must recognize that these strengths, like people in general, are not infallible.

In all of my personal research and observations about self-awareness and "knowing strengths," I have been motivated by numerous others in the professional development, leadership, and goal-setting fields. Notably, Michael Hyatt provides perspective on the other side of the coin: weaknesses.

In his article "Why You Should Understand Your Weaknesses," Hyatt argues that knowing one's weaknesses is just as important as knowing one's strengths in the pursuit of greater happiness and productivity. Why would this be? He writes that, in identifying weaknesses, you avoid "engaging in activities where you can't make much impact." After all, we cannot be good at everything. We can only be great at a few things.

Additionally, this focus on weaknesses, he acknowledges, provides opportunities to know and elevate other people who have within them the very strengths that you are missing—*your* weaknesses. In turn, this strengthens the engagement, contributions, happiness, and productivity of the whole team. Furthermore, by taking stock of one's weaknesses and not just avoiding them wholesale, internal frustrations (*why am I not getting better at this?*) are minimized. And when you are less exasperated, odds are that your team and loved ones who surround you will also be less frustrated.

MASTERING SELF-MANAGEMENT

When discussing vital leadership competencies within the MSC framework, consultant J. P. Flaum walks us through his leadership acceleration firm's history with helping organizations recruit and develop top leaders. Flaum also sheds light on the ways that the perception of the personality characteristics and qualities most beneficial to CEOs is undergoing a positive evolution.

Much of what one may still consider to be a helpful strength in a productive executive may require a makeover, especially as organizations seemingly always have plenty of projects to take on to clean up messes resulting from bad executive hires. In the report "When It Comes to Business Leadership, Nice Guys Finish First," Flaum introduces readers to "Steve," the exec who proudly "doesn't sugarcoat."

As with many accomplished executives, the outcomes achieved by Steve and his team came at a high cost. He was smart and hard-charging, but his style was often harsh, impulsive, and mercurial. Within six months of his hiring, the company was faltering. Two senior staff members exited. Others' feet were partially out of the door. Impulsive changes to projects had wreaked havoc with development schedules. A considerable opportunity—one that promised an acquisition of a major software company—was falling through because of suddenly "uninspired product features" and "unfulfilled promises" and because "[the software firm's] executive vice president in charge of acquisitions found his conversations with Steve to be such an unpleasant experience."

Flaum continues, "Last week, one of the software firm's clients saw a board member at a social event and complained that Steve was painful to work with, and 'didn't seem forthright.' The hiring committee is wondering how they could have gotten it all so wrong."

What society has often gotten wrong is the picture of the harsh, hard-charging, take-no-prisoners, results-at-all-costs executive. He doesn't care much for others' feelings and disregards "soft skills."

But he wins the loyalty of boards, investors, and clients due to driving results. So, the thinking goes, results matter and the staff's happiness, feelings, motivation, and sense of being needed are only distractions "from what really matters: the bottom line."

Flaum concluded that this is a recipe for disaster and, furthermore, that this thinking "isn't remotely true, even when focused solely on growth, profitability, ROI, and other core financial metrics." As Flaum expresses it:

> In fact, executives who lack interpersonal skills—executives who just focus on numbers and processes and wreak havoc on their people—perform poorly over all but the shortest of time periods. And their businesses do as well. This is a verifiable fact. Executives who are bullies—who are arrogant, "too direct," impatient or stubborn—are poor performers, not only as people managers, but also at developing strategy and delivering bottom-line financial results.

On the other hand, executives characterized as good "people managers" who possess strong core leadership skills

> produce better strategic and financial performance outcomes. In other words, **soft values drive hard results**. . . . **We don't mean pushovers or "doormat executives" either.** We mean leaders who are self-aware, able to hold teams accountable, and who can execute tough decisions in an inspiring and fair—not abusive—manner. We also mean executives who encourage rather than snuff out productive conflict and the challenging of ideas—even their own. [Emphasis in original.]

And what came of Steve? Flaum recalls that his exit was "messy, painful, and costly." Steve's successor, "Joyce," has her "work cut out for her." There are teams that must be rebuilt from the ground upward, and there is morale that must be restored. Outside the walls of the firm, client relationships and business partnerships must be repaired. Strategic direction will also need to be clarified, with new "road maps" put in place to account for the disarray in product scheduling. But there is reason to be hopeful. Joyce tested well for people skills. "With luck," Flaum writes, "Steve's tenure will turn out to be a detour—and another blow to the idea that you can be bad with people and still be good at business."

A NEW-SCHOOL APPROACH

Joyce embodies the true executive/leader strengths as quantified by Anthony K. Tjan, an author, entrepreneur, and strategic advisor whose team developed the Entrepreneurial Aptitude Test found on his website for *Heart, Smarts, Guts, and Luck,* the book he coauthored with Richard Harrington and Tsun-yan Hsieh. "There is *one* quality that trumps all, evident in virtually every great entrepreneur, manager, and leader," Tjan writes in his article "How Leaders Become Self-Aware." "That quality is self-awareness. . . . Without self-awareness, you cannot understand your strengths and weaknesses, your 'super powers' versus your 'kryptonite.'"

Accordingly, the Entrepreneurial Aptitude Test measures how entrepreneurs, managers, or leaders stack up in one of four key traits that drive business and entrepreneurial success, all of which align with the title of Tjan's book: heart, smarts, guts, and luck.

In a blow to the old-school "who cares about your feelings?" leader, Tjan shared that across a set of 500 global entrepreneurs and business builders, about *half* of those who took the test were found to be "heart-dominant," with the remaining 25 percent "luck-dominant" and 15 percent and 10 percent "guts-" and "smarts-dominant," respectively.

For further insights into the qualities behind each of these types, I turn to the online home of *Heart, Smarts, Guts, and Luck*:

- **Heart-dominant**—These leaders are often some combination of founder, iconoclast, or visionary. They possess traits of authenticity, deep caring, and a drive to translate passions into reality and to make changes that are bigger than one's product or team.
- **Guts-dominant**—Decisiveness and bold action are right in these leaders' wheelhouse. They never experience any of the difficulties others are weighed down with when making a tough or unpopular decision. They lead, manage, and motivate as a "starter," with the capacity to endure and persevere during challenging times.
- **Smarts-dominant**—Often described as bright, intellectually driven, and highly talented, managers who lead from their smarts ("book," "street," or otherwise) are all connected in their ability to navigate decisions with clear-eyed, rational thinking and analysis no matter what. In turn, such leaders possess a better-than-average capacity to recognize and consider patterns when making decisions.
- **Luck-dominant**—While it may seem that some people stumble upon fortuitous circumstances and are just plain lucky, Tjan and his team have determined that luck-dominant individuals are also defined by a set of core attributes. These attributes are defined as the "Lucky Attitude" and the "Lucky Network." The former is characterized by humility, intellectual curiosity, and optimism, whereas the latter is characterized by those relationships that occur outside of formalities— by-products of spending time with individuals with whom there is mutual esteem.

A thread running throughout our modern-day exploration of MSC in this book is a defiance of the boundaries that formerly characterized our perceptions of certain types of people, relationships, programs, or processes. This exploration of core competencies is no different; no longer should self-reflection, self-awareness, and "soft skills" or "people skills" be marginalized. They are absolutely essential to the well-being of profitable organizations, healthy societies, and local communities alike.

Regardless of the assessment, the practice of self-coaching—the consistent, intentional investment of time and effort toward living a life of reflection and examination—results in a deeper knowledge of self that informs our journey and forms us into the leaders that we aspire to be. In order to lead others well, we must first lead ourselves well. The practice of self-coaching is an invaluable investment toward that end.

KEY TAKEAWAYS

- One effective way to engage in coaching is to practice self-coaching: the intentional investment of time and effort toward reflection and a consistent examination of our lives and leadership for continued growth and improvement.
- Self-coaching can be solitary, but it can also involve connections and community with trusted colleagues.
- Self-awareness is a primary objective of self-coaching. The most effective leaders know themselves and lead themselves well.
- Self-coaching involves nurturing an acute knowledge of our strengths and weaknesses and of how they impact and influence our life and leadership.

REFERENCES

Batista, E. 2018. "Self-Coaching Is SOCIAL." EdBatista.com. Published May 28. http://edbatista.com/2018/05/self-coaching-is -social.html.

Flaum, J.P. 2013. "When It Comes to Business Leadership, Nice Guys Finish First." Green Peak Partners. Updated May 8. http://greenpeakpartners.com/wp-content/uploads/2018/09/Green-Peak_Cornell-University-Study_What-predicts-success.pdf.

HSGL.com. 2022. "Entrepreneurial DNA Profile Results." Accessed November 1. http://www.hsgl.com/entrepreneurial_aptitude_test_overview.php.

Hyatt, M. 2010. "Why You Should Understand Your Weaknesses." FullFocus.co. Published August 11. http://fullfocus.co/why-you-should-understand-your-weaknesses.

Tjan, A. K. 2012. "How Leaders Become Self-Aware." *Harvard Business Review*. Published July 19. http://hbr.org/2012/07/how-leaders-become-self-aware.

Tjan, A. K., R. J. Harrington, and T. Hsieh. 2012. *Heart, Smarts, Guts, and Luck: What It Takes to Be an Entrepreneur and Build a Great Business*. Boston: Harvard Business Review Press.

CHAPTER 11

Core Competencies

As I HAVE guided you through different ways to partner with others to develop your personal and professional acumen, certain coveted and healthy characteristics have surfaced again and again within all of these developmental networks and relationships. Researchers have naturally boiled these core competencies down to a science. Some of these strengths can further be distilled into an understanding of our unique individual weaknesses themselves, which moreover illustrate the importance of "bigger picture" self-awareness.

In *Skills for Successful Mentoring: Competencies of Outstanding Mentors and Mentees*, the strategy booklet authored by the late Dr. Linda Phillips-Jones, effective relationships on this front were conveyed as more than common sense or that "mysterious 'chemistry.'" In her prolific research, Phillips-Jones concludes that these successful relationships demonstrate many specific and identifiable skills. Some of these skills are shared by both mentors and mentees ("core skills"), whereas others ("critical skills") are unique to the mentor or the mentee.

CORE SKILLS

Core skills include the following:

- Active listening
- Encouragement

- Identification of goals and the current reality
- Building trust

Active listening presents the foundation upon which other skills are built. It means that mentors or mentees know their concerns are being heard and understood, which further promotes some of the other qualities noted in the Phillips-Jones competency lists, such as acceptance and trust.

Numerous observable behaviors are part of active, quality listening; for example, the mentor or mentee may paraphrase certain comments made during the conversation. This shows that you have a grasp of the meaning behind the other participant's words, and it helps provide a fresh, forward-thinking twist that further advances the discussion.

Naturally, frequent interruptions are the enemy of active, thoughtful listening. Sincere follow-up questions and summaries of key elements are foundational to this process, and you should avoid turning the conversation back on your own experiences. In fact, doing so can be detrimental to the process of providing an open outlet for the other person to share and convey personal experiences, thoughts, challenges, scenarios, or aims.

> The process of active listening is often challenging for high achieving professionals, as it's a muscle we flex less frequently in our day-to-day lives, where we're more consistently called on to be decisive, give direction, and to have the answers.

There is power in the capacity to *wait* for answers after the question is asked and to not always have answers at the ready. It is vital that each person arrives at their own discoveries and enlightenment and that the savvy leader gently nudges them toward self-awareness and introspection. There is also considerable psychological safety fostered within this dynamic. While leaders are often paid to be decisive and to have all of the answers and solutions, the successful and high-performing leader-coach knows that they were given two ears and one mouth for a reason. Shut the latter, engage the former.

The second of Phillips-Jones's core, shared skills is **encouragement**, which involves sincerity in providing positive feedback (or "feedforward"). Phillips-Jones suggests that one err on the side of *too much* praise rather than too little: "Some human development experts recommend a ratio of four or five praises for every corrective remark."

The core competency of **identification of goals and current realities** involves a clear definition of the visions, dreams, and professional and personal life goals right alongside the reality at present—of-the-moment strengths, limitations, and situations or circumstances within one's workplace and/or household. From there, partners can work together to determine the specific resources or assistance that is needed to rise to such a vision, dreams, and goals within the current context. Phillips-Jones recommended setting tentative short-, mid-, and long-term objectives. Throughout this journey, fresh feedback is regularly incorporated.

Lastly, the core competency of **trust** further breeds commitment to the partnership. Specific actions foster trust and, accordingly, commitment to the process: keeping conversations confidential, respecting each other's precious time (and prioritizing engagements within these partnerships), following through on promises, drawing boundaries and keeping within them, admitting errors, taking responsibility, and exercising tact when disagreements or dissatisfaction inevitably creep into even the most healthy and amicable of relationships. All of these characteristics are particularly important when dealing with any "cross-differences," such as differences in genders, cultures, generations, or personality styles.

The awareness and acknowledgment of cross-differences also hearkens back to my earlier discussion of overcoming barriers in the process by considering how input or observations can best be incorporated by the other person. While certain insights may have worked for you, will they work for someone who is not identical to you in background, station, or journey? Are you not checking a bias or privilege, which in turn makes your counsel or experience inapplicable or irrelevant (or worse, offensive?) In appreciating these differences and accounting for them at every turn, you create a level of respect and conscientiousness that breeds trust and sustained commitment.

In Stephen R. Covey's seminal book on trust, *The Speed of Trust: The One Thing That Changes Everything*, the legendary businessman-author-motivator-educator asserts that trust is not just a "touchy-feely" quality that is nice to have. It's a hard-nosed business asset that delivers quantifiable economic value.

The higher the trust factor, the greater the level of execution on deliverables and the lower the costs, he argues, noting that it makes good financial sense to consistently find methods to enhance the levels of trust inside and outside a business organization. Covey encourages readers to visualize the effect of trust as ripples created by a droplet of water falling into a pool. The drop generates concentric circles that always flow from the center outward. Following through on the metaphor, Covey isolates "Five Waves of Trust." Each wave represents a way in which trust is established.

The first wave concerns self-trust: an individual's ability to set and achieve goals and to maintain commitments. The second wave relates to relational trust, which concerns the trust that an individual firms up and increases with others. The third wave, organizational trust, involves making a splash among others to get more done and is derived from an alignment of values within an organization. Market trust, the fourth wave, is driven by the reputation of the organization's brand, while the fifth wave, societal trust, places value on others and society writ large, with the ultimate goal of contributing to both in meaningful and positive ways.

Covey ascertains that the "pragmatic, tangible, actionable asset" of trust is itself derived from certain specific competencies:

- Being selective in those whom you trust
- Having the capacity to restore lost trust by not being quick to judge and by prioritizing forgiveness
- Acting on the natural propensity to trust others, which defies the notion of the rather "jaded" CEO or senior professional and leads one to get in touch with one's inner, idealistic, or past self

MENTOR-CRITICAL SKILLS

Pivoting to those unique skillsets that were defined as "critical" to mentors, these characteristics are as follows:

- Instructional and developmental capabilities
- Inspirational qualities
- Providing corrective feedback
- Risk management
- Opening doors

Instructional and developmental capabilities often include informal guidance and the modeling of specific behaviors by the mentor for the mentee. It is the mentor's responsibility to connect the mentee to resources and broader perspectives that are beyond the mentee's scope and reach. These resources might include institutional knowledge as to the history or politics within one's organization or workplace.

Inspirational qualities are really what separates the good mentor from the great mentor. Connect the dots between the mentee and other inspiring people, resources, and situations. Arrange for highly motivating experiences, and challenge the mentee to "rise above the mundane," tackling important activities and responsibilities within organizations or communities.

Providing corrective feedback can be tricky; mentorship scholars suggest being as direct as possible when communicating one's perceptions and equipping the mentee with suggestions on alternative ways to handle situations. Since this can be a slippery and uncomfortable slope, all healthy mentor-mentee relationships should first start with the mentor asking the mentee, "Would you like feedback?" If the answer is yes, then the natural follow-up should be "How would you like to get feedback?" This presents a guide you can both use throughout the partnership, and it also aids in setting expectations and managing risks. Be positive, not disparaging. Be specific, not wishy-washy.

Risk management is no small feat. Much is at stake every day, as any leader's performance and credibility affects future potential. Hence, it is critical that a mentee be equipped to take on only *appropriate* risks. Mentors are invaluable sources of counsel during an assessment of problematic circumstances or tough decisions.

Opening doors is embodied by an "activated ally" or sponsor. In the broader context of MSC partnerships, it is vital for the mentor to know which door is the right one for the mentee. A little bit of legwork goes a long way, in that the mentor should be willing and able to "talk up" the mentee before introductions to appropriate contacts, assignments, resources, and opportunities (the "doors").

MENTEE-CRITICAL SKILLS

Phillips-Jones identifies the following as critical mentee-specific skills:

- Acquiring mentors
- The ability to learn quickly
- Showing initiative
- Following through
- Management of the relationship

Mentees, resist the temptation to be unassuming or passive when **acquiring mentors**. Be active when identifying and engaging with *multiple* mentors. As noted previously, each person has entire circles of friends, acquaintances, and professional contacts. What may serve one well now may not serve one's career stage or circumstances in the near-term or long-term future. Mentors rarely have a lot of time on their hands, so the responsibility falls on mentees to be as specific as possible about what they are looking for in terms of the relationship. Concrete and actionable goals, needs, expectations, time frames, confidentiality considerations, feedback processes, and meeting schedules must all be discussed and agreed upon.

The ability to learn quickly is invaluable in all workplaces, sectors, and industries. It is a must for the mentor to see mentees as willing and passionate about learning, able to get ramped up fast, and interested in taking the process very seriously. It is critical to observe the "role model" mentor carefully and closely, to integrate observations into one's day-to-day life and problem-solving methods, and to demonstrate and communicate that such learning was seamlessly applied within the workplace.

Few attributes are more appreciated in mentees than **initiative.** Many mentee-specific competencies flow from this characteristic. The key is to not sit back and let the opportunities or the mentor (with all of their obligations and responsibilities) come to you. With that being said, a balance should be observed in showing the *right amount* of initiative. After all, there is a difference between being enthusiastic about the opportunities and partnership and being overzealous within the relationship. One must continue to be cognizant and respectful of the mentor's time and bandwidth.

Following through concerns a hard truth: It will likely always be a "mentor's market" because of the very nature of the mentorship process. If a mentee doesn't follow through on promises or steps within the goal-seeking and strengths-building relationship, they will be dropped and replaced with an individual who is serious and committed. When Phillips-Jones polled mentors, they expressed frustration in a mentee's inability to follow through with agreed-upon tasks. The frustration was so irksome that *many mentors refused to enter new mentoring relationships because of this experience.* Mentees, you do matter, and you can have ripple effects far beyond a single relationship. Do not be the failed mentee who is at the root of the following statement: "I was working harder on the mentee's life than they were!"

In mentorship, sponsorship, and coaching, each relationship is unique, so it's always helpful to clarify objectives, expectations, and progress. Successful partnerships require intentional **relationship management**. Be sure to mind every step in the "life cycle" of the relationship. Be aware that all relationships can morph and even end. Take note of this potential from the get-go in order to foster a supportive and amicable dissolution of the formal relationship while acknowledging that conversations can continue informally in perpetuity. One thing is certain: classic etiquette is never out of style. The wise mentee, sponsee, or coachee is always gracious and grateful. We almost never achieve greatness alone. The counsel and company that others lend to us is one of life's richest blessings. When we generously turn around and share the same blessings with others, we perpetuate a cycle of positive influence and expertise-building.

KEY TAKEAWAYS

- Core competencies for mentors, sponsors, and coaches include active listening, building trust, encouragement, and identifying goals and current standing.
- The process of active listening is often challenging for high achieving professionals, as it's a muscle we flex less frequently in our day-to-day, when we're called on to be decisive, give direction, and to have the answers.
- Important actions that mentors, sponsors, and coaches can take include instruction, inspiration, delivering corrective feedback, identifying and managing risks, and opening doors.
- Critical mentee skills include acquiring mentors, the ability to learn quickly, showing initiative, following through, and managing relationships.

REFERENCES

Covey, S. M. R. 2008. *The Speed of Trust: The One Thing That Changes Everything.* New York: Free Press.

Phillips-Jones, L. 2003. "Skills for Successful Mentoring: Competencies of Outstanding Mentors and Mentees." CCC/The Mentoring Group. Published November 5. http://my.lerner.udel.edu/wp-content/uploads/Skills_for_Sucessful_Mentoring.pdf.

CHAPTER 12

Putting It into Practice

ACCORDING TO MERRIAM-WEBSTER, *culture* is "the set of shared attitudes, values, goals, and practices that characterizes an institution or organization." Throughout this book, I have referenced "cultures" in nearly the same breath as successful mentorship teams and organization-wide professional development. Too often, we think of development in terms of fleeting programs. We do not think in terms of the long-term attributes that are integrated into the very fabric of organizations and workplaces.

This shortsightedness applies to all areas of business—from programs exclusively targeted at decreasing the rates of risk factors for costly and serious disease to programs designed to increase the use of 401(k) plans and other key employee benefits as a means of fostering financial well-being. However, with so much riding on talent to promote positive health outcomes, meet severe labor shortages across industries, and foster overall societal wellness, advancing professional development deserves so much more than mere programming, a singular initiative, or rote steps.

In addition, as Stefanie K. Johnson and David R. Hekman assert in the *Harvard Business Review,*

As organizations seek to reflect the broader societies in which they operate, increasing racial and gender balance is becoming more urgent. The harsh reality discussed here highlights the importance of putting appropriate structures and processes in place to guarantee the fair evaluation of women and minorities. The challenge of creating equality should not be placed on the shoulders of individuals who are at greater risk of being crushed by the weight of this goal.

This statement suggests the need for diverse attributes that are interwoven into culture—the standards and structures, processes and policies—as well as the additional implications of designing a culture of healthy development and mentorship and recognizing its urgency in the current environment. Another key takeaway from a review of the leadership development and mentoring research is the need to hire and onboard for those skills that align with the successful, modern leader and executive.

Greater care must be taken when selecting, promoting, and investing in first-time managers, as well as seasoned managers who may be considered "executive material" or who may have served as executives elsewhere. Keep in mind that varied experience at different companies is not always a good sign. As J. P. Flaum puts it, it may instead be indicative of an executive who is hopping about from employer to employer, trying to outrun a problem. "That problem often has to do with how they 'fit' in the workplace. Job hoppers also lack perspective on the outcome of their leadership decisions, as they typically leave before the changes take effect."

When the organization has developed these structures and cultural attributes, and they are unshakable within the fabric of the workplace, the practices that support healthy and equitable recruitment, promotions, learning, and growing are seamless. The organization has the framework to buttress these processes and approaches.

CULTURE: THE ENGINE OF ORGANIZATIONAL SUCCESS

As reported by workplace design and research firm Haworth, the notion of "organizational culture" was popularized in the 1980s. This time frame, incidentally, coincided with the popularization and celebration of the Gordon Gekko–style corporate raider who took no prisoners, glorified greed at all costs, and would decidedly not fare well in today's assessments of core competencies held by successful leaders.

Haworth researchers point out that "organizational culture has increasingly come to be understood as an asset to enhance performance":

> Culture is often difficult for an organization to articulate, but its impact is far reaching and influences management, process, products, employee attraction and retention, reputation, and ultimately the bottom line. . . .
>
> No matter how strong an organization's planned procedures, culture trumps strategy when the two are not aligned. The best strategic concept won't work in isolation, especially if it conflicts with the overarching culture of a company.

Culture is often described as the glue that holds organizations together, the compass that provides direction, or simply "the way we do things around here." Indeed, David G. Smith and W. Brad Johnson, authors of *Athena Rising: How and Why Men Should Mentor Women*, developed a piece whose title sums up the importance of mentoring as a facet of company culture: "Real Mentorship Starts with Company Culture, Not Formal Programs." The duo, often enlisted to support diverse mentoring cultures for firms around the globe, examine the assumption that merely having a mentorship program is the cure for all that ails the floundering, disengaged, underperforming workforce:

> Ask executives and managers how junior talent is encouraged, developed, and supported, and you'll hear some variation of this refrain: 'We've got a mentoring program!' Even vague rumors of a mentoring 'program' nested somewhere in HR allow too many leaders to check off the employee engagement and development blocks without carefully scrutinizing the quality, utilization rates, and outcomes of such formalized mentoring structures.

Pointedly, Smith and Johnson assert that the problem is in programs that typically rely on individual mentor–mentee matches: the formal and hierarchical pairings mentioned in chapter 5. There is a disconnect between these pairings and the evidence, which tells us that many employees prefer a more reciprocal and mutually beneficial relationship.

Furthermore, the authors state that even the best programs are not likely to achieve intended outcomes, because the workplace may be competitive and individualistic. Senior leadership may only engage in developing juniors when they are being pursued by prospective mentees or are being "volun-told" to participate within a formal framework.

"Mentorship programs alone won't sufficiently engage or develop your junior talent, especially if your culture doesn't encourage mentoring on a regular basis," Smith and Johnson write. "What your company needs instead are *mentors-of-the-moment*" (emphasis in original).

As explored in chapter 5, such a model flips the script on the staid, onerous, "add-on" obligation that so often characterizes traditional mentoring programs. There are many small moments throughout the day that can represent opportunities for real, viable connections and growth—be it a simple passing of a colleague in the corridor, a greeting of a visitor to the office, or an informal chat around the watercooler. All of these situations present the potential, outside of formalities and programming, to commend individuals on excellent contributions, to ask about the next steps in their careers or projects, and to counter that performance-inhibiting "impostor syndrome" with just the right positive affirmation at just the right time, when an employee may have needed it the most.

What an organization is trying to do by breaking free of the confines of programs and "box-ticking" is to integrate "micro-exchanges" into its culture. Smith and Johnson describe this process as an "exposure effect in social psychology" with valuable micro-exchanges building informal and increasingly bonded mentoring relationships. They contend that even relatively brief interactions can lead to transformative developmental relationships.

It is little wonder, then, that employees prefer organic or informal mentorships to forced or otherwise arbitrarily assigned programs with a firm structure. To aid in creating a mentoring culture, Smith and Johnson suggest several recommendations:

- **Use simple conversation starters.** I often suggest that prospective mentors make the little comments that can lead to big, impactful growth and connections. These starters could be as straightforward and off-the-cuff as "Hey, I noticed your great work on _____. Great job!" Or one could solicit the high-performer's insights with the following comment: "I'm working on _____. What do you think? I'd value your perspective."
- **Talk them up.** Career milestones or achievements should not be allowed to pass by without acknowledgment. One is doing one's team, organization, and culture considerable good by highlighting these milestones and accomplishments for others. It breeds belonging and validation, and it can lead to increased "mission-critical" work opportunities for the individual so deserving of the notice.
- **Take feedback (or feedforward).** In addition to refining the art of giving regular, well-thought, and positive feedback, one should also be open to *receiving* feedback. I understand that sometimes receiving insights from peers

or even those who are our juniors can be a difficult pill to swallow; however, remember that a feeling of defensiveness can be a symptom of a barrier to workforce performance and wellness: hubris and ego. A learning, mentoring, successful culture is built on mutuality, reciprocity, and trust.

- **Sustain clarity, transparency, and accountability.** Smith and Johnson cite the work of behavioral economist Iris Bohnet when addressing the fundamentals to changing a culture to one of mentorship and healthy and effective professional development. Bohnet argues that there are "three pillars" to change.

    The first pillar, *clarity*, is about making the connection between daily mentoring behaviors and the broader good of the employees and workplace over the longer term. The second pillar, *transparency*, involves identifying and communicating the "hows" and "whys" that inform essential workplace interactions, intentionally setting aside time and resources, and supporting frequent mentoring exchanges. The third pillar, *accountability*, is marked by holding specific individuals accountable for promoting and assessing mentoring culture (the "metrics"). Evaluations should include questions on day-to-day activities that foster cultural improvement, as well as tasks that track overall progress and ensure direct reports are accountable for the behaviors that inform cultural change.

- **Identify future mentors from the get-go.** Recruit and promote next-gen leaders on the basis of the characteristics that make them so well suited to mentoring. This is very much a proactive stance, in that one is vetting candidates for certain mentor-friendly attributes and behaviors rather than hoping they'll be engaging as a mentor simply because they hold a formal leadership role in the organization.

    Look for a proclivity for "prosocial" behaviors that benefit others (such as helping, sharing, or providing comfort), a caring orientation, and great communication skills. The language that is used during the hiring process should reflect this priority; for instance, ask the applicant, "How do you inspire and support others around you? When was the last time that you helped a junior colleague? What did you do and why?"

- **Keep a finger on the pulse of the mentoring culture.** Metrics are important. Consider that old chestnut, "What gets measured, gets managed." Do not wait for annual reviews. The mentoring culture—and improvements or changes made to it—should be assessed regularly. Assessments may involve conducting anonymous polls of junior, midlevel, and senior leadership.
- **Positively reinforce, and even reward, mentoring behaviors.** Positive reinforcement is an effective training method. Use it! To increase the frequency and quality of desirable mentoring behaviors within a workplace culture, use findings from assessments or other ongoing metrics to shout out high-performers in the mentoring realm publicly. Invest in rewards, putting one's money where one's mouth is, to fund honors that celebrate the most prolific talent developers and "star-makers."

By emphasizing mentors-of-the-moment and micro-exchanges rather than perfunctory assigned relationships, Smith and Johnson further note how the culture or behaviors "embedded in the workplace DNA" now better support inclusivity and the acceptance and active engagement of diverse experiences and conversations. On this front, the Smith/Johnson duo emphasize evidence-based strategies in another report that appeared in the *Rutgers Business Review*: "Male Allies Must Publicly Advocate and Sponsor."

These strategies to hone and sustain a diverse, gender-equitable mentorship culture ranged from being a raving fan and nominating women for promotions (not waiting for them to do so), to providing cover and sharing "social capital" (defined as resources like advice, goodwill, influence, knowledge, and support).

For example, Smith and Johnson recall how Jen Welter's ascension to become the NFL's first female coach has inspired others to follow suit. Coach Bruce Arians had to take a risk on Welter as an NFL "first" for the floodgates to open and to make this type of ascendancy for women more culturally acceptable. The 2021 season was historic in its unprecedented volume of women serving as coaches in the league. A total of 12 women serve in roles ranging from assistant running back coaches to strength and conditioning coaches.

Smith and Johnson's call to action:

> Inclusion-minded male leaders move forward to engage in deliberate and equitable sponsorship, it's often helpful to do an honest audit and ask, "Am I boldly sponsoring some high-potential employees?" If so, "Does everyone I sponsor look like me?" Be intentional about diversifying those you pull up and push forward. Become creative and deliberate about finding junior women to sponsor. It's not only good for women, it sets up your organization for success.

As leaders, we have a unique opportunity. Whether we simply lead ourselves, a team or project, or an entire organization, our actions set the standard and can impact the culture. Mind that impact!

I'd also like to challenge the prospective mentee, sponsee, or coachee to balance thinking inward with thinking outward: consulting one's supporters, considering how one's actions align with and reinforce the good of the team or organizational culture, and evaluating one's individual objectives for growth and impact.

Just as identifying profitability-enhancing "people" or soft skills and "teachability" from the get-go is important, it is also important to position each engagement and mentorship opportunity for success from the outset. Think in terms of each and every conversation,— and the words that are used in each and every conversation, especially the initial "ask."

One must have the confidence and wherewithal to solicit someone's expertise, but remember not to ask, "Will you be my mentor?"

(which sounds silly when verbalized outright). Ask instead to bend the potential mentor's ear—a *conversation* rather than a *relationship* or commitment. Know what to ask for within each conversation.

It is never easier for a mentor to say yes than when you, as the prospective mentee, clearly define objectives and expectations. For instance, ask your prospective mentor, "Can I get 20 minutes of your time to talk about two specific questions?" In the "ask," you are clear, effective, and efficient, in stark contrast to the less effective, inefficient "cold call"-style of mentor solicitation. You, as the mentee, must be willing to do the heavy lifting, especially when first establishing these connections. Be proactive, prepped, reflective, and flexible.

Also, if one conversation doesn't lead to something more, consider soliciting one or two connections within that person's network. Here's a script I like to suggest: "Based on what you've learned about my objectives from our conversation today, who are one or two other individuals in our organization or your network whom you think I might benefit from having a conversation with?" You never know who you may benefit from. While the prospective mentor conversation may not result in the partnering you had initially hoped for, meeting with a member of the prospect's network very well could blossom into something mutually beneficial and fruitful. Be gracious and respectful of each person's time and understand that building trust and rapport takes time.

In all MSC relationships, prioritize nurturing psychological safety and the vulnerability to openly discuss insecurities, graciously accept and integrate feedback, and to set goals. This requires both courage to face one's weaknesses or flaws and the maturity and self-awareness to know there is always room to grow. Own these imperfections as well as the potential that mentors can draw out of you by empowering you within formal and informal conversations.

Half cheerleader and half drill sergeant, mentors have keen vision in identifying and pulling more out of their charges than what those charges thought they had in them. Few things are more satisfying and rewarding.

> "Good mentors help us to get close to our full potential."
> —Dr. Kimberly Manning

Imagine an army of "good mentors," willing mentees with the right skill sets, and a willingness to invest in MSC that sees the concept not as a collection of disparate, underperforming company programs but rather as a philosophy that nurtures performance-driven cultures. Healthy cultures built on the right interfaces and dynamics of individuals with the right skill sets can result in the organizational, industry-wide, communal, and societal transformations that have eluded us throughout history.

As leaders, the ideal strategy for impact is to surround ourselves with circles of people who will pour into us, and then to consistently share that with those who are around, ahead of, and behind us. Mentors, sponsors, and coaches are examples of excellence and of the formal and informal teaching and community that imbue our continual growth.

I hope that upon partaking of this book, you feel encouraged and better equipped to put the practices of mentorship, sponsorship, and coaching to work for your edification and that of others around you.

Go forth in growth, my friends.

KEY TAKEAWAYS

- For organizations that aspire to be more diverse, equitable, and inclusive to reflect the communities they serve, cultural change is essential to better recruit, develop, advance, and retain leaders who can rise to that challenge.
- Hire for, onboard, promote, and recognize the people whose skills align well with a culture of mentorship, sponsorship, and coaching.

- A culture of mentorship will outperform a mentorship program every time.
- A culture of mentorship nurtures and encourages the organic mentoring exchanges that are meaningful and sustainable.
- When seeking a mentoring relationship, don't ask for a mentoring relationship—it's a big commitment. Rather, ask for a conversation with a specific objective. If the conversation is a good one, consider asking for another.
- As a mentee, do the heavy lifting. Be proactive, well-prepared, reflective, and flexible. If you make it easy for someone to be your mentor, they'll be more likely to do so.
- Be gracious and respectful of your mentor's time.
- Building rapport takes time. Trust and psychological safety are requisite foundations for the vulnerability to discuss insecurities and opportunities for growth.

REFERENCES

Bohnet, I. 2016. *What Works: Gender Equality by Design*. Cambridge, MA: Belknap Press.

Flaum, J. P. 2013. "When It Comes to Business Leadership, Nice Guys Finish First." Green Peak Partners. Updated May 8. http://greenpeakpartners.com/wp-content/uploads/2018/09/Green-Peak_Cornell-University-Study_What-predicts-success.pdf.

Haworth. 2015. *How to Create a Successful Organizational Culture: Build It—Literally*. Published June 15. http://media.haworth.com/asset/55249/How%20to%20Create%20a%20Successful%20Organizational%20Culture.pdf.

Johnson, S. K., and D. R. Hekman. 2016. "Women and Minorities Are Penalized for Promoting Diversity." *Harvard Business Review*. Published March 23. https://hbr.org/2016/03/women-and-minorities-are-penalized-for-promoting-diversity.

Johnson, W., and D. Smith. 2021. "Male Allies Must Publicly Advocate and Sponsor." *Rutgers Business Review* 6 (2): 137–144.

————. 2019. "Real Mentorship Starts with Company Culture, Not Formal Programs." *Harvard Business Review*. Published December 30. http://hbr.org/2019/12/real -mentorship-starts-with-company-culture-not-formal-programs.

Manning, K. 2012. "Mentors." *ACP Hospitalist* (blog). Published July. http://acphospitalist.acponline.org/archives/2012/07/blog .htm.

About the Author

Laurie K. Baedke, MHA, FACHE, FACMPE, is a faculty member at Creighton University, where she serves as the program director for the CAHME-accredited Executive MBA in Healthcare Management program in the Heider College of Business and as the assistant dean of Physician Leadership Education in the School of Medicine.

A frequent speaker at international healthcare conferences and facilitator at company and association retreats, Laurie works with teams and individuals that include early careerists, physician leaders, and senior executives. She has specific expertise in physician practice management, leadership development, organizational change, emotional intelligence, and strengths-based leadership.

Laurie holds a bachelor's degree in human services and business administration and a master's degree in healthcare administration. She is a Fellow of the American College of Healthcare Executives (ACHE) and of the American College of Medical Practice Executives, as well as a member of the Medical Group Management Association. She has been certified by Gallup as a strengths performance coach since 2006.

Laurie is the recipient of numerous awards, including the Nebraska ACHE Regent's Early Career Excellence Award (2001), the District Five ACHE Regent's Award for Healthcare Excellence (2006), and the ACHE Distinguished Service Award (2015).

Professionally, she has served on four national ACHE committees: the Early Careerist; Programs, Products and Services; Chapters; and Examination committees. She also serves a variety of civic and community organizations, including the Omaha Bridges Out of Poverty, where she is appointed to the board of directors executive committee.

Laurie lives just outside of Omaha, Nebraska, with her husband and two children.